TEACH YO

GW00385537

GENERAL LINGUISTICS

Linguistics is the scientific study of language; it attempts to answer the fundamental questions 'what is language?' and 'how does it work?'. This book is intended as a straight-forward introduction to linguistics for those approaching this fascinating and fast-expanding field of study for the first time. It outlines the scope of linguistics, explaining basic concepts and essential terminology with illustrations drawn mainly from English. Sound patterning, grammar and meaning—the bread and butter of linguistics—are discussed simply and clearly, and there are also chapters on historical linguistics, psycholinguistics and sociolinguistics, as well as suggestions for further reading.

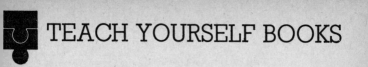

TEACH YOURSELF BOOKS

GENERAL LINGUISTICS

Jean Aitchison, M.A., A.M.

Lecturer in Linguistics, London School of Economics

ST. PAUL'S HOUSE   WARWICK LANE   LONDON EC4P 4AH

First printed 1972
Second impression 1973
Third impression 1974

Copyright © 1972

The English Universities Press Ltd.

ISBN 0 340 12467 9

*Printed by photolithography and made in Great Britain for
The English Universities Press Ltd. at The Pitman Press, Bath*

CONTENTS

PART FOUR. SOME RECENT DEVELOPMENTS

PREFACE

This book is an introduction to introductions to linguistics.

There are several books on the market which call themselves 'introductions' to the subject, but which are in fact more suited to second year students.

This book is to help people working by themselves to break into the 'charmed circle' of linguistics. It explains basic concepts and essential terminology.

It is not a bedside reading book, and contains no chatty anecdotes. It is a straightforward handbook for those who wish to know about the subject. Linguistics is a highly technical field, and technical vocabulary cannot be avoided.

Linguistics is a field torn apart by controversies. Wherever possible, this book takes a 'middle-of-the-road' view. Not that a middle-of-the-road view is necessarily right, but it is possibly more helpful for those new to the subject.

Hopefully, readers will view this book as a stepping stone to some of the works suggested in the bibliography—books such as John Lyons's *Introduction to Theoretical Linguistics*, which provides stimulating insights into many of the problems currently under discussion among linguists.

Teach Yourself General Linguistics is intended to complement Robert Lord's *Teach Yourself Comparative Linguistics*. Consequently, several topics that are adequately dealt with in that book are omitted from this (e.g. survey of the language families of the world, writing systems).

I am very grateful to all those who have made helpful suggestions and comments—in particular Professor John Lyons of Edinburgh University, Dr. J. Buse of S.O.A.S., London University, and Mr. Christopher Ball of Oxford University.

However, this book does not in any way represent their views, as I have not always followed their advice.

J.A.

ACKNOWLEDGMENTS

For permission to include copyright material in this book the author and publishers are grateful to the Estate of the late Sir Alan Herbert for a passage from *What a Word* by A. P. Herbert; to J. M. Dent & Sons Ltd. for lines from 'This is my own, my native language' by Ogden Nash from *Collected Verse From 1929 On*; and to Dr. J. B. Searle for his limerick 'There was a young man of Dunlaoghaire'.

PART ONE

GENERAL INTRODUCTION

Worry about words, Bobby. Your grandmother is right. For, whatever else you may do, you will be using words always. All day, and every day, words matter. Though you live in a barrel and speak to nobody but yourself, words matter. For words are the tools of thought . . .

A. P. Herbert

CHAPTER 1

What is Linguistics?

The average human being spends an immense amount of his life talking, listening, and (in advanced societies) reading and writing. Normal conversation uses 4000 or 5000 words an hour. A radio talk (where there are fewer pauses) uses as many as 8000 or 9000 words per hour. A man reading at normal speed covers 14 000 or 15 000 words per hour.

So someone who chats for an hour, listens to a radio talk for an hour and reads for an hour possibly comes into contact with 25 000 words in that time. Per day, the total could be as high as 100 000.

Speech and the ability to think abstractly are closely connected. These two characteristics above all separate humans from animals. All over the world, babies learn to talk at approximately the same age and follow re-markably similar patterns of development.

Psychologists are realising that inability to use language adequately can fundamentally affect a man's personality. Teachers, speech therapists, sociologists, anthropologists, communications engineers, journalists and advertising men are all beginning to realise that they need to study language more deeply.

So it is not surprising that in recent years one of the fastest expanding fields of study has been general lin-guistics—the scientific study of language.

Linguistics tries to answer the basic questions 'What is language?' and 'How does language work?'.

It probes into various aspects of these problems,

such as 'How does human language differ from animal communication?', 'How does a child learn to speak?', 'How does one write down and analyse an unwritten language?', 'Why do languages change?'.

What is a Linguist?

A person who studies linguistics is usually referred to as a **linguist.** The more accurate term 'linguistician' is too long and pompous to become generally accepted. The word 'linguist' causes confusion, since it also refers to someone who speaks a large number of languages.

A linguist (a linguistics expert) need not be fluent in languages, though he must have a wide experience of different types of languages. It is more important for him to be able to analyse and explain linguistic phenomena such as the Turkish vowel system, or German verbs, than to make himself understood in Istanbul or Berlin. He is a skilled, objective observer rather than a participant.

A linguist is best likened to a musicologist. A musicologist could analyse a piano concerto by pointing out theme and variations, harmony and counterpoint. But he need not play the concerto himself. He leaves that to the concert pianist. Music theory bears the same relation to actual music as linguistics does to language.

Why is Linguistics a Science?

Most academic disciplines pass through three stages in their development.

First comes a stage of speculation. People have speculated about language for centuries. In the Middle Ages it was commonly believed that all languages were descended from Hebrew, a claim based on the Bible. The Old Testament was written in Hebrew, so this was the language that Adam and Eve must have spoken in the Garden of Eden, it was claimed.

Secondly, there comes a stage of observation and classification. Minute observation, and the systematic collection and cataloguing of facts characterise this phase. Such work starts off without any preconceived notions and is objective rather than subjective. Nineteenth century scholars considered that this objectivity allowed a discipline to rank as a science. So linguistics has been called a 'science' for more than a hundred years.

But conscientious amassing and cataloguing of data is insufficient by itself. And a discipline which is a true science has reached a third stage, the **formulation of hypotheses.**

A discipline at this stage understands the basic problems involved in its study and asks questions about these problems. For example, a linguist might ask what universal features of grammar underlie the languages of the world. Then it formulates hypotheses, or theories, which attempt to answer the questions raised, and tests the facts against such hypotheses.

It does not matter how a hypothesis is arrived at: it could be via a dream, or by chance. Newton proposed the theory of gravitation when an apple fell on his head. What does matter is the careful testing of the hypothesis against the data. In order to be acceptable, a theory must be **exhaustive, consistent** and **economical.**

An exhaustive theory is one which accounts for all the facts. A consistent theory is one in which there are no internal contradictions. An economical theory is one which is as simple and straightforward as possible. If a theory does not fulfil these three criteria, it must be rejected or amended.

Linguists, then, are engaged in the formulation of

theories as to how language (or bits of language) works. For this reason, linguistics can be defined as 'the scientific study of language'. It is regarded as one of the social sciences, alongside such subjects as psychology and sociology.

How does Linguistics differ from Traditional Grammar?

One frequently meets people who think that linguistics is old school grammar jazzed up with a few new names. But it differs in several basic ways.

Firstly, and most important, linguistics is **descriptive,** not prescriptive. A linguist is interested in what IS said, not what he thinks ought to be said. He describes language in all its aspects, but does not prescribe rules of 'correctness'.

It is a common fallacy that there is some absolute standard of correctness which it is the duty of linguists, schoolmasters, grammars and dictionaries to maintain.

There was an uproar in America in 1961 because *Webster's Third New International Dictionary of the English Language* included words such as *ain't* and phrases such as *ants in one's pants*. The editors were deliberately corrupting the language—or else they were incompetent, argued the critics. 'Webster III has thrust upon us a dismaying assortment of the questionable, the perverse, the unworthy and the downright outrageous', said one angry reviewer.

But if people say *ain't* and *ants in one's pants*, a linguist considers it his job to record the fact. He is an observer and recorder of facts, not a judge.

'I am irritated by the frequent use of the words *different to* on radio and other programmes', ran a recent letter to the *Evening News*. 'In my school days of fifty years ago we were taught that things were *alike to* and *different from*. Were our teachers so terribly ignorant?'

Languages are constantly changing. And the fact that a writer comments on the **frequent** use of *different to* indicates that it has as much right to be classified as 'correct' as *different from*.

Another common fallacy is the insistence on avoiding 'split infinitives' as in the phrase *to humbly apologise*, where the infinitive *to apologise* is 'split' by *humbly*. A letter to the *Evening Standard* is typical of many: 'Do split infinitives madden your readers as much as they do me?', asks the correspondent. 'Can I perhaps ask that, at least, judges and editors make an effort to maintain the form of our language?'

The idea that a split infinitive is wrong is based on Latin. Purists insist that, because a Latin infinitive is only one word, its English equivalent must be as near to one word as possible. To linguists, it is unthinkable to judge one language by the standards of another. Since split infinitives occur frequently in English, they are as much 'correct' English as unsplit ones.

The notion of absolute and unchanging 'correctness' is quite foreign to the linguist. He might recognise that one type of speech appears, through the whim of fashion, to be more socially acceptable than others. But this does not make the socially acceptable variety any more interesting for him than the other varieties.

A second important way in which linguistics differs from traditional school grammar is that linguists regard the **spoken** language as primary, not the written.

In the past, grammarians have overstressed the importance of the written word, partly because of its permanence. It was difficult to cope with fleeting utterances before the invention of sound recording.

Partly also the traditional classical education was to blame. People insisted on moulding language in accordance with the usage of the 'best authors' of classical times—and these authors existed only in written form. This attitude began as far back as the second century B.C. when scholars in Alexandria took the authors of fifth century Greece as their models. This belief in the superiority of the written word has continued for over two millennia.

But linguists look first at the spoken word, which preceded the written everywhere in the world, as far as we know. Most written languages are derived from the vocal sounds and are therefore secondary. (There are a few exceptions. One is Chinese, where one written language links together vastly different spoken systems.)

Spoken language follows a different set of rules from the written. In linguistics, spoken and written forms are regarded as belonging to different (though overlapping) systems, which must be analysed separately.

A third way in which linguistics differs from traditional grammar studies is that it does not force languages into preordained categories. The world is split up differently by every language. Tense categories such as past, present, future are by no means universal. One frequently meets languages which do not have this distinction. Instead, they might distinguish between the type of action involved, specifying whether it was a recurring action, a continuing action or a single action.

It was assumed for a long time that Greek and Latin grammars provided a universal framework into which all languages would fit. This is a fallacy. Countless schoolchildren have been confused by meaningless attempts to force English into these patterns. But English structure is totally different. It does not have nominatives, accusatives, datives, etc. It is untrue to say that *for John* is in the 'dative case', since English does not have a Latin-type case system.

Ideally, a linguist approaches every new language

with an open mind, and without any preconceived notions about parts of speech, tenses, cases, etc. He describes each language on its own terms, and only sets up categories that he has deduced from the internal structure of the language.

There may well be certain universal grammatical features which all languages have in common. This is a topic under heated discussion at the moment. But, so far, these universal features are far from obvious, and preconceived notions can only complicate matters.

The Scope of Linguistics

General linguistics covers a wide range of topics and its boundaries are difficult to define.

A diagram in the shape of a wheel gives a rough impression of the range covered.

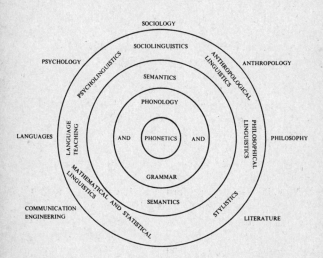

In the centre is **phonetics,** the study of human speech sounds.

A good knowledge of phonetics is essential for a linguist. Yet it is a basic background knowledge, a prerequisite for linguistics rather than part of linguistics itself. Just as you must learn to read before studying literature, so you must have a knowledge of phonetics before studying linguistics.

A phonetician is concerned with the actual physical sounds, the raw material out of which language is made. He studies the position of the tongue, teeth and vocal cords during the production of sounds, and records and analyses sound waves.

A linguist is more interested in the way in which language is patterned. He analyses the shape or **form** of these patterns rather than the physical **substance** out of which the units of language are made.

The famous Swiss linguist, Ferdinand de Saussure, expressed the difference well when he compared language with a game of chess. The linguist is interested in the various moves which the chessmen make and how they are aligned on the board. It does not matter whether the chessmen are made of wood or ivory. Their substance does not alter the rules of the game.

Although phonetics and linguistics are sometimes referred to together as 'the linguistic sciences', phonetics is not as central to general linguistics as the study of language patterning. For this reason, phonetics is dealt with mainly in the Appendix in this book.

Phonology (sound patterning), **grammar** and **semantics** (meaning) are the 'bread and butter' of linguistics. They are the central concern of this book. Semantics is placed outside phonology and grammar because of its closer connection with the external world.

Around this central core are the various branches

of linguistics which are being rapidly developed at the present time: **psycholinguistics, sociolinguistics, anthropological linguistics, philosophical linguistics, mathematical linguistics, stylistics** and **language teaching.**
Adjacent to these, but outside the circle, are the disciplines to which these branches of linguistics are most closely connected.

QUESTIONS

Test yourself on what you have read in Chapter 1 by answering the following questions:

1. How would you define linguistics?
2. Why is linguistics referred to as a **science?**
3. What is the difference between a **prescriptive** and a **descriptive** approach to language?
4. Why do linguists regard **speech** rather than writing as primary?
5. Why is a Latin framework unsuitable for English grammar?
6. Explain the difference between **form** and **substance.**

CHAPTER 2

What is Language?

General linguistics has been defined as 'the scientific study of language'—a discipline which describes language in all its aspects and formulates theories as to how it works.

But what exactly *is* language? How does one define it? What are its characteristic features?

One of the best ways to begin to answer this question is to compare language with animal communication, and to see where the similarities and differences lie.

Medium of Communication

When animals communicate with each other, they may do so by means of touch, smell, sight or sound.

Three-spined sticklebacks, for example, use visual signals. A female stickleback is attracted to the male because of his red belly and bright blue eyes. Some baby birds ask for food by pecking at a red patch on their mother's beak.

The male of certain species of moth is attracted to the female because of the odour she emits—and he will even attempt to mate with a sheet of paper impregnated with this odour.

But such signals are not as widespread as sound signals, which have the great advantage of being able to be used in the dark. This may be the reason why we (and other animals such as grasshoppers, birds, dolphins and monkeys) have preferred this medium.

Man probably acquired his sound signalling system at a fairly late stage in his evolution. This seems likely because all the organs used in speech have some more basic function.

The lungs are primarily used for breathing. Teeth, lips, and tongue are primarily for eating.

The vocal cords (thin strips of membrane deep in the throat) were used primarily for closing off the lungs in order to make the rib cage rigid for actions requiring a great effort. When a man lifts something heavy, he automatically holds his breath. This is caused by the closing of the vocal cords. The grunt when the heavy object is dropped is the air being expelled as the vocal cords open. Millions of years ago man needed a rigid rib cage for swinging in the trees—but humans still need this mechanism today for actions such as weight-lifting, defecation and childbirth.

Arbitrary Nature of Language

There is often a strong link between the actual signal and the message an animal wishes to convey. An animal who wishes to warn off an opponent may simulate an attacking attitude. A cat, for example, will arch its back, spit and appear ready to pounce.

In human language, the reverse is true. In the great majority of cases, there is no link whatsoever between the signal and the message. The symbols used are **arbitrary.** There is no intrinsic connection, for example, between the word *elephant* and the animal it symbolises. Nor is the phrase 'These bananas are bad' intrinsically connected with food.

Onomatopoeic words such as *quack-quack* and *bang* are exceptions—but there are relatively few of these compared with the total number of words.

Scope of Reference

Most animals can communicate about things in the immediate environment only. A bird utters its danger cry only when danger is present. It cannot give information about something which is removed in time and place. This type of utterance is nearer to a human baby's emotional cries of pain, hunger or contentment than it is to fully developed language.

But human language can communicate about things that are absent as easily as about things that are present.

This apparently rare phenomenon, known as **displacement,** occurs also in the communication of honey bees. If a worker bee finds a new source of nectar, he returns to the hive and performs a complex dance in order to inform the other bees of the exact location of the nectar, which may be several miles away. But even bees are limited in this ability. They can inform each other only about nectar. Human language can talk about any subject whatever, no matter how far away the topic of conversation may be.

Acquisition

Most animals automatically know how to communicate without learning. Their systems of communication are genetically inbuilt. Bee dancing, for example, is substantially the same in bee colonies in different parts of the world, with only minor variations.

Possibly there is a minor element of learning involved. A chaffinch reared in a soundproof room away from other chaffinches developed an abnormal type of song. Yet when the bird was exposed to only occasional tape recordings of other chaffinches, its song developed normally.

This is quite different from the long learning process needed to acquire human language, which is **culturally**

transmitted. A human being brought up in isolation simply does not acquire language—as is shown by the rare studies of children brought up by animals without human contact.

But human language is by no means totally conditioned by the environment. There is certainly some type of innate predisposition towards language in a new-born child, otherwise all languages would be far more dissimilar. But this latent potentiality can only be activated by long exposure to language, which requires careful step-by-step learning.

Variety of Message

Most animals have a very limited number of messages they can give or receive. The male of a certain species of grasshopper, for example, has a choice of six, which might be translated as follows:

1. I am happy, life is good.
2. I would like to make love.
3. You are trespassing on my territory.
4. She's mine.
5. Let's make love.
6. O how nice to have made love.

Bees can communicate only about sources of nectar. Dolphins have a high intelligence, and a large number of clicks, whistles and squawks—but even they do not seem to be able to say anything new.

Great efforts have been made to teach animals to speak.

Some years ago an American couple tried to bring up a chimp called Viki as if it were a baby. They gave Viki intensive coaching in how to talk. But after three years she could say only three words: *papa*, *mama*, *cup*. She could respond to simple commands such as *kiss me*, and eventually she was able to obey more complex commands such as *kiss your hand*—but the result was very disappointing compared with the speech of a human five year old (the equivalent of a three year old chimp).

More recently, a chimp called Washoe has been taught to use sign language. She has a repertoire of over sixty signs and can use them in the right situations. She is beginning to combine signs into simple phrases, such as *open—food—drink* to mean 'Open the refrigerator' when she is hungry or thirsty.

Yet another chimp, a Californian animal called Sarah, is claimed by its teacher to be learning language. She has a vocabulary of over one hundred words, it is reported, and by manipulating signs on a slate can make sentences such as *Sarah insert apple dish* 'Sarah puts the apple into the dish'.

Both these animals appear to have the ability to create new combinations of symbols—and this is a remarkable achievement. But, compared with the language ability of a human child, the results are negligible.

A human can produce an incalculable number of new combinations from the elements of his language. He can utter sentences which he has never uttered before and be understood. If someone said 'There is a purple platypus crawling across the ceiling', his friends might think he was drunk or drugged, but they would understand him.

In addition, language can cope with entirely new situations by adding new items: *sputnik*, *astronaut*, *moon rocket*, *radar* are all relatively recent additions to the English language.

Only human language, it seems, is capable of dealing with unforeseen and novel situations in this way. This **productivity,** as it is called, appears to be absent or very limited in animal communication.

Organisation of Sounds

Animals who use vocal signals have a stock of basic sounds which vary in number according to species. A cow has under ten, a chicken has around twenty and a fox over thirty. Dolphins have between twenty and thirty, and so do gorillas and chimpanzees.

Most animals can use each basic sound only once. That is, the number of messages an animal can send is restricted to the number of basic sounds, or occasionally the basic sounds plus a few simple combinations.

Each human language has a stock of sound units or **phonemes** which are similar in number to the basic sounds possessed by animals. The average number is between thirty and forty.

These phonemes are in themselves meaningless, but they are combined into larger meaningful units or **morphemes.** The number of possible morphemes is enormous—an educated man might use up to 100 000, according to one calculation.

This organisation of sounds into two layers, one of phonemes and one of morphemes, is known as **duality** or **double articulation.**

Duality means that language is a much more powerful tool than animal communication systems, since the mathematical possibilities of combinations of morphemes are incalculable.

These combinations follow careful rules. Man does not use thousands of sound combinations at random. Instead, he rings the changes on a few well-defined patterns.

Human Language versus Animal Communication

So far, the main similarities and differences between human and animal communication can be summarised as follows.

Human language is a signalling system which uses

sounds, a characteristic shared by a large number of animal communication systems.

In animal communication, there is frequently a connection between the signal and the message communicated, and messages about absent objects and events are possible only in exceptional circumstances. In human language, the symbols are mainly arbitrary and the topic of conversation is frequently absent.

Human language has to be painstakingly transmitted from one generation to another, while learning appears to be of subsidiary importance in animal signalling.

The ability to say new things (productivity) is almost totally absent from animal communication, but is an essential feature of language. Duality and strict rules of patterning may well be unique language characteristics, with no parallel in the animal world.

So we may define language as **a patterned system of arbitrary sound symbols, whose characteristic features of displacement, cultural transmission, productivity and duality are rare or absent in animal communication.**

This is true of all languages in the world, which are remarkably similar in their main design features. There is no evidence that any language is more 'primitive' than any other.

There are certainly primitive cultures. A primitive culture is reflected in the vocabulary of a language, which might lack words common in advanced societies. But vocabulary is superficial. Even the most primitive tribes have languages whose underlying structure is every bit as complex as English or Russian or Chinese.

Origin and Functions of Language

Language, as we have seen, is a highly developed form of animal signalling. But there is a missing link in the chain. How, and when, did we start to talk?

This is a problem of interest to ethologists (students of animal behaviour) and psychologists, and one which has not yet been solved. Most linguists regard this fascinating topic as being outside the realm of linguistics proper. They are more interested in studying actual language than in speculations about its remote origins.

But although *how* language began is a puzzle, *why* language began seems rather clearer.

It possibly began because men needed a greater degree of co-operation with each other in order to survive, and this co-operation required efficient communication.

Consequently, the primary function of language is to impart factual information, or convey essential commands. This is sometimes called the **directive** function of language, or, more simply, information talking.

But language can also be used to communicate feelings and emotions, the so-called **expressive** function of language, or mood talking. This aspect of language is not as well developed as information talking. This is partly because man can convey his emotions by screams, grunts, sobs, gestures and so on, so he needs language only to confirm and elaborate these more primitive signals.

In addition, there is the language of social chit-chat, the meaningless small talk of everyday life. 'Hallo, how nice to see you. How are you? Isn't the weather terrible?' This social patter has been called **phatic communion** and is primarily a device to maintain social contact on a friendly level. Some ethologists call it grooming talking and suggest that it is a substitute for the friendly grooming indulged in by monkeys.

There are other less important functions of language. A man may use language for purely aesthetic reasons. In writing poetry, for example, he manipulates words in the same way as he might model clay or paint a picture.

Or he may talk in order to release nervous tension, a function seen when people mutter to themselves in anger and frustration.

Language Patterning

Language has been defined as a patterned system of arbitrary sound symbols.

Perhaps the most striking aspect of language is its patterning. As has been said, man does not store thousands of different sound combinations in his head haphazardly. Every utterance follows strict rules of patterning. A linguist tries to discover these rules.

Every item in a language has its own characteristic place in the pattern, a place which is different from that of every other item. An item's place in the pattern can be discovered by examining, firstly, the items which normally occur in combination with it and, secondly, the items which can replace it.

An item has a **syntagmatic** relationship with the items which can occur in combination with it:

c ← a → t   the ← cat → caught a mouse

An item has a **paradigmatic** relationship with any item which can replace it:

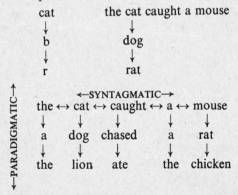

By studying the syntagmatic and paradigmatic relationships of each item, it is possible to build up a picture of its distribution, that is, its own characteristic place in the pattern.

Structural Linguistics

The elements of language are like the players in a game of football. A left-half, or a goal-keeper, has no use or value outside the game, and his position and movements are entirely dependent on the position and movements of the other players.

The whole of language is an intricate network of patterning in which every item is held in its place and given its identity by all the other items. No item has an independent validity or existence outside that pattern.

Ferdinand de Saussure (1857–1913) was the first person to point out clearly that language was not a haphazard heap of individual items, but a highly organised **structure** in which all the elements are interdependent. He repeatedly likens language to a game of chess in which each chessman's role is entirely dependent on the positions of the other chessmen on the board. From him we date the era of 'structural linguistics'.

This realisation of the interlinked nature of language is the basis of modern linguistics.

The term 'structural linguistics' is sometimes misunderstood. It does not in general refer to a separate branch or school of linguistics. *All* linguistics since de Saussure is structural, as structural in this sense merely means the recognition that language is a patterned system composed of interdependent elements rather than a collection of unconnected individual items. Misunderstandings arise as certain American linguists of the 1950s are sometimes termed 'structuralists' because of their preoccupation with the way items were arranged to form a total structure, to the exclusion of all other aspects of linguistics.

Language is Always Changing

A game of chess or a game of football provides a useful analogy for language. These games illustrate clearly the interdependent nature of the various elements.

But, in another way, such analogies falsify the situation. They give a spurious impression of neatness and tidiness with their set number of players and well-defined boundaries.

All languages are always changing. One of the greatest strengths of any language is the fact that it can cope with novel situations by inventing new words and new combinations of words.

But this means it is constantly in a state of flux. And, because all the elements are interlinked, a change involving one element affects every other element.

Within language, there is an automatic self-regulating device. If changes occur, either they fit into existing patterns or new patterns are formed to fit in with the changes. Whatever happens, language must remain patterned, otherwise communication would break down. It is the patterning which enables a man to remember so many items and say so many things. His memory could not cope with a jumbled confusion of thousands of items.

Because of this state of flux, the patterns of language are never perfect. There are always jagged edges and exceptions. As the American linguist Edward Sapir said, 'All grammars leak'.

Constant change and leakiness make things difficult for the linguist. He must treat language as a self-contained interlocking system—yet at the same time recognise that this system has fuzzy edges and is continually (though slowly) changing.

QUESTIONS

1. Why does it seem likely that man developed language at a fairly late stage in his evolution?
2. What is meant by **productivity?**
3. What is meant by **duality?**
4. Distinguish between **syntagmatic** and **paradigmatic** relationships.
5. What is meant by **structural** linguistics?

CHAPTER 3

The Study of Language: Greeks—Twentieth Century

Before the nineteenth century, language in the western world was of interest mainly to philosophers. It is significant that the Greek philosophers Plato and Aristotle made major contributions to the study of language.

To begin with, the Greeks were more interested in the origin of language than in analysing it.

Discussions on the origin of language set up a major controversy between two opposing views: those who believed in the 'natural' origin of language versus those who believed in a 'conventional' origin.

The 'naturalists' believed that there was by nature a correct name for everything. They pointed out that a number of words were onomatopoeic, such as *cuckoo*, and that others had a 'natural' connection with their meaning. Words denoting movement, for example, frequently contained an *r*, a sound which appeared to denote movement in its articulation. (The Greek words for *run, flow, tremble* all contain *r*.)

The 'conventionalists' ridiculed this theory. They asserted that the names for things were due purely to convention and had no deep appropriateness. (This is the viewpoint held by linguists today. See Chapter 2.)

This dispute is discussed at length in Plato's *Cratylus*. To linguists today such an argument may seem pointless. But the Greeks were still influenced by a primitive belief in the magic properties of names. In primitive societies, a thing *is* its name, and this magic link is unbreakable. So the naturalists were supporting a deep-rooted attitude—an attitude which is still found surprisingly often even in advanced societies.

In addition, the Greeks had little systematic knowledge of other languages. They bundled all non-Greek speakers together under the name *barbaroi* 'people who say bar-bar, people who talk gibberish'. So they could not appeal to another language to solve their arguments.

Alongside such speculations and disputes, grammatical analysis was begun. Plato is said to have been the first person to distinguish between nouns and verbs.

But it was not until the third century B.C., the so-called Hellenistic era, that scholars at Alexandria produced competent grammars of Greek in which tense, mood, case, gender and other traditional categories were fully dealt with. The most famous is the grammar of Diony-sius Thrax, written in the second century B.C.

The city of Alexandria was the centre of intensive academic activity at this time. Above all, texts of the famous classical Greek authors were studied, corrected and edited.

This preoccupation with the great authors of classical Greece encouraged the fallacy that the language in which they wrote was in some way better and purer than current-day speech. Scholars tried to prevent the 'corruption' of the Greek language from spreading by condemning any usage which differed from that of these old masters.

For the same reason, there arose a great reverence for the written word. It was the twentieth century before linguists freed themselves from this obsession and started to study spoken before written language (see Chapter 1).

The Romans copied the Greeks slavishly in all aspects of linguistic scholarship. Grammars of Latin were fitted into a Greek framework. This was not such a serious fault, as Greek and Latin do to some extent fit into the same pattern. But it had serious repercussions in that it encouraged people to think that this framework was a universal one, to be used as a basis for writing grammars in all languages.

The most famous Latin grammars are those by Donatus (c. 400 A.D.) and Priscian (c. 500 A.D.), which were used as standard text books as late as the Middle Ages.

Middle Ages and After

In the Middle Ages, a number of scholars known collectively as the **Modistae,** or **speculative grammarians,** made the most notable contribution to the study of language.

The name Modistae was attached to them because they produced numerous works entitled *De Modis Significandi* 'concerning the ways of signifying'. Their other name, the speculative grammarians, is from the Latin word *speculum* 'mirror'. It arose from the assumption that language in some way reflects a reality which underlies the physical world of objects. Their prime concern was to find out the nature of the relationship between words and this reality. Such a belief led to the search for universals in grammar, on the assumption that all grammars are basically the same and only differ superficially. This view has recently been revived, and it is one of the most controversial topics in linguistics today.

Printing was invented in the mid-fifteenth century. After this, there was a dramatic increase in the amount of material available for language study. There were several attempts to make comprehensive collections of languages and to survey all languages then known.

This re-aroused interest in the origin of language. One

much-discussed problem was whether or not all languages came from a single source. A popular view was
that Hebrew was man's original language. This was the
language given to Adam by God in the Garden of
Eden. Man's language remained uniform until the build-
ing of the Tower of Babel. Then God in his anger
'confounded' the languages of the world and made men
unable to understand one another.

A few unnoticed scholars attempted to provide less
fanciful reconstructions of language history, but their
work was largely ignored. The period is more important
for the amassing of information than for new ideas.
In addition, the renewal of interest in Greek and Latin—
and particularly Latin, the language of the Church—
resulted in new refinements in the writing of grammars
and editing of texts.

William Jones (1786) and the Nineteenth Century

1786 is one of the most important dates in the history of
linguistics. An Englishman, Sir William Jones, read a
paper to the Royal Asiatic Society in Calcutta pointing
out that Sanskrit (the old Indian language), Greek,
Latin, Celtic and Germanic all had striking structural
similarities. So impressive were these likenesses that
these languages must spring from one common source,
he concluded. (Although Jones has the credit of making
this discovery, it was an idea that was occurring independently to several scholars at the same time.)

Sir William Jones' discovery fired the imagination of
scholars, and historical linguistics became a major
preoccupation for the next hundred years.

Nineteenth century linguistics can be split into three
major phases. For the first half, linguists concentrated on
writing detailed comparative grammars—grammars com-

paring the different grammatical forms of the various members of the Indo-European language family:

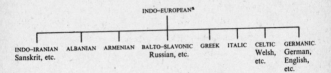

Halfway through the century, an important event occurred. In 1859, Darwin published his *Origin of Species*, stating the theory of evolution. This had repercussions on all fields of scholarship.

In linguistics, it inspired scholars to try to reconstruct the original **Proto-Indo-European** language, the ancestor from which the various Indo-European languages were descended. It also misled other scholars into trying to chart the development, maturity and decline of languages.

The most enthusiastic of these Darwinian scholars was a German named Schleicher, who attempted to translate one of·Aesop's fables into reconstructed Proto-Indo-European. Schleicher viewed his reconstructed language as representing a language in a mature and undamaged state, the culmination of thousands of years of development. All subsequent changes he regarded as symptoms of decline and decay. (Such beliefs about 'states of development' are now regarded as unfounded. See Chapter 6.)

In the last quarter of the century, a major controversy split the linguistic world. This was due to a group of scholars centred round Leipzig who were known as the **Junggrammatiker** or Neogrammarians.

The basic tenet of the young grammarians was that 'sound laws are regular'. If a sound changes, then it

[1] HITTITE and TOCCHARIAN have been recognised as Indo-European languages in the twentieth century.

changes whenever it occurs in the same phonetic environment, at the same time and in the same geographical area. Such 'laws' operated by 'blind necessity', independent of the will of any individual.

This statement aroused great opposition. The Neogrammarians claimed to have discovered a universal principle, akin to natural laws such as the laws of gravity.

Older and more conservative scholars objected to the sweeping nature of the Neogrammarians' claim—and they pointed out numerous exceptions to these so-called 'laws'.

Today, the basic assumption of the Neogrammarians is an accepted part of linguistic theory. But undoubtedly the word *law* is an unfortunate choice for describing systematic sound changes. Physical laws do not stop and start in the same way as sound laws, which work for a given time and then cease operating. In addition, certain factors can prevent the working of sound laws (see Chapter 11)—though many of the apparent exceptions quoted in the nineteenth century were due to insufficient knowledge of the conditions surrounding certain changes. Further research caused the laws to be modified and the exceptions disappeared.

Twentieth Century: De Saussure

In the nineteenth century, linguists were interested primarily in historical linguistics: the history of languages, language change and the reconstruction of Proto-Indo-European.

In the twentieth century, the emphasis shifted to synchronic (descriptive) linguistics.

If any one person changed the emphasis of linguistics in Europe it was the Swiss scholar Ferdinand de Saussure (who has already been mentioned several times). After his death in 1913, his students collected together his lecture notes and published them under the title *Course in General Linguistics* (1915).

De Saussure stressed three important points. Firstly, descriptive linguistics must be distinguished from historical linguistics and the two approaches coped with separately. This is an extremely useful methodological principle, and it enabled language description to be freed from discussions of historical development (see Chapter 4).

Secondly, de Saussure distinguished between *langue* (language) and *parole* (speech). By *langue*, Saussure meant a language viewed as a whole, the abstract system which imposed itself on every speaker. *Parole*, on the other hand, referred to an actual physical utterance. The distinction is a useful one, since it recognises the need for idealisation and abstraction, as well as concern with actual data (see Chapter 4).

De Saussure's third contribution is his most important. He pointed out the structural nature of language, the fact that its elements are essentially interlinked. These elements are not a random collection of spare parts, but the function of each one is determined by its relationship with all the others. To illustrate this he used his famous metaphor likening language to a game of chess. It is the relationship of each chessman to the other chessmen which is the essence of the game (see Chapter 2).

Twentieth Century: Daniel Jones and the Phoneme

Phonetics, the study of speech sounds, received particular attention towards the end of the nineteenth century and the beginning of the twentieth. Interest was at first centred on the development of an efficient system of phonetic notation. Various systems were invented and tried out. The first version of the International Phonetic Alphabet (I.P.A.) was published in 1888. This is the system most widely used in Europe. It has been progressively improved since its introduction and is now an effective (though obviously imperfect) instrument for the transcription of most languages. It has never been widely adopted in America, where several systems are in use. This is unfortunate, as the lack of an overall American system causes confusion both to Americans and to Europeans.

An interest in phonetics led to an interest in phonology. Linguists gradually realised that an intricate pattern of significant sound units, or phonemes, underlay the sounds of any language (see Chapter 5).

Theories surrounding the phoneme caused violent disputes. Was the phoneme an abstract entity, having a purely psychological reality? Or was it a concrete entity, with a physical reality which could be recorded and measured?

English scholars have always been to the forefront in phonetics and phonology, particularly those based in London. One of the most important figures in the development of the concept of the phoneme was Daniel Jones, who taught at University College, London, for more than forty years.

In the late 1920s and 1930s, a group of scholars centred round Prague initiated a different type of work on the phoneme. They tried to analyse each phoneme into its component parts or features. Their aim was to pinpoint the features which distinguished each phoneme from all the others. This type of work is known as **distinctive feature** theory and is a major part of the work going on in phonology at the present time (see Chapter 5).

Another interesting approach to phonology was pioneered by J. R. Firth, the first professor of general linguistics at London University. In most analyses, words were regarded as a sequence of individual phonemes. Firth, in his system known as **prosodic analysis,** pointed out that this approach was not always satisfactory. Quite often, some important phonetic feature lasted for several phonemes. So he emphasised the need for studies within phonology which would cope with this problem. Firth's prosodic phonology has not been generally adopted, though it is better known in England than elsewhere. For this reason, there is no further mention of it in this book.

Firth's second important contribution to linguistics was his attempt to deal with the meaning of an utterance within its social setting or **context of situation** (see Chapter 9).

But linguistics in Britain was slow getting established as a subject. Consequently, Firth's views were only handed on to a few enthusiastic pupils and have not influenced the general trend of linguistics internationally to any great degree.

Twentieth Century: Bloomfield and the Americans

In America, linguistics developed far faster than in Britain. This was largely due to the presence of numerous American-Indian languages. These were fast becoming extinct, and scholars rushed to record them before it was too late.

Anthropologists began this American-Indian campaign, and to a large extent linguistics began in America as an offshoot of anthropology. The most famous anthropologist-sociologist-linguist was Edward Sapir, whose book *Language* (1921) is still an excellent introduction to linguistics.

Leonard Bloomfield, whose major work was also entitled *Language* (1933), initiated a new era in American linguistics. Up till then, much descriptive work had been haphazard and lacking in cohesion. Bloomfield attempted to lay down a rigorous framework for the description of languages.

Bloomfield considered that linguistics should deal objectively and systematically with observable data. So he was more interested in the forms of a language than in meaning. The study of meaning was not amenable to rigorous methods of analysis and was therefore, he concluded, 'the weak point in language study, and will remain so until human knowledge advances very far beyond its present state'.

Bloomfield had immense influence, and many standard text books are based largely on his work. But his pessimism over the possibility of dealing with meaning led to its neglect by many American scholars.

The so-called 'Bloomfieldian era' lasted for more than twenty years. During this time, American linguistics became obsessed with the problem of extracting a grammar from a mass of data. Linguistic items were identified and classified without reference to meaning, as far as was possible, by studying their distribution within the data.

These problems were important, and a valuable background of linguistic methodology was laid down for future generations.

But linguistics also became very narrow. Trivial problems of analysis became major controversial issues, and no one who was not a linguist could understand the issues involved. Linguistics lost touch with other disciplines and became an abstruse subject of little interest to anyone outside it. It was ready for a revolution.

Chomsky

In 1957, linguistics took a new turning. Noam Chomsky, then aged twenty-nine, a teacher at the Massachusetts Institute of Technology, published a book called *Syntactic*

Structures. Although containing fewer than 120 pages, this little book revolutionised the study of linguistics.

Chomsky's contribution was twofold. Firstly, he questioned the accepted goals towards which linguistic theory was oriented, and redefined the aims and functions of a grammar. Secondly, he specified the form this new-type grammar should take. It was to be a **transformational** grammar.

Chomsky and transformational grammar are the subject of Chapter 8.

QUESTIONS

1. What was the **nature** versus **convention** controversy of the ancient Greeks?
2. Who were the **Modistae?**
3. Why is **Sir William Jones** important in the history of linguistics?
4. Who were the **Junggrammatiker,** and what was their main contribution to linguistics?
5. Why is **de Saussure** an important figure in linguistics?
6. What are the main characteristics of **Bloomfieldian** linguistics?

PART TWO

ANALYSING LANGUAGE

Alice was too much puzzled to say anything, so after a minute Humpty Dumpty began again. 'They've a temper, some of them—particularly verbs, they're the proudest—adjectives you can do anything with, but not verbs—however, I can manage the whole lot!'

Lewis Carroll

CHAPTER 4

Cutting Language Up

Language covers an immense range. So linguists have to make a number of artificial cuts in order to divide it up into more manageable chunks.

Descriptive versus Historical Approach

One of the most basic of the artificial cuts made by linguists is the division between descriptive and historical linguistics.

Descriptive (or **synchronic**) linguistics studies a language at a single point of time. It concentrates on the state of a language and completely ignores all the processes which led up to that state.

A descriptive linguist is like a photographer who petrifies a group of people in a certain position—and forgets what went before and after the taking of the picture.

Historical (or **diachronic**) linguistics studies language change—and all languages are continually changing.

The difference between descriptive and historical linguistics can be illustrated by the now classic diagram of Ferdinand de Saussure, who was the first person to stress the necessity of distinguishing between the two approaches.

In the diagram, axis AB is the synchronic, static axis. It can intersect at any point with CD, the moving, diachronic axis.

Some people assume that historical studies form the most important part of linguistics. This is an old-fashioned view which arose because nineteenth century scholars concentrated almost exclusively on this aspect of language. They were particularly concerned with comparative historical linguistics (or comparative philology)—a branch of historical linguistics which compares the various forms of related languages and attempts to reconstruct the mother-tongue from which they all developed.

In the first half of the twentieth century, the pendulum swung the other way. Descriptive linguistics almost displaced historical linguistics. Particularly in America, detailed descriptive accounts of the remaining American-Indian languages have, until relatively recently, been a major preoccupation.

In a sense, historical linguistics depends on descriptive linguistics. Any diachronic account of a language must be based on a careful examination of a number of descriptive studies spread over a wide time range. For this reason, descriptive linguistics is dealt with before historical linguistics in this book.

Competence and Performance

One of the most obvious (and one of the most astonishing) facts about language is that every speaker appears to have the grammar of his language internalised in his brain so that he can automatically recognise and reject an ungrammatical sentence such as 'Quickly table green under happy'. At the same time, he can understand and form an infinite number of completely new sentences—sentences which may never have been uttered before.

If someone says 'Purple elephants are turning somersaults in the hall', you would understand him, even though you might never have heard this sentence before.

The abstract, internal grammar which enables a speaker to utter and understand an infinite number of potential utterances is referred to as a speaker's **competence** (a term suggested by Chomsky).

Since competence is an abstract, internal system, we need another word to describe the actual utterances a speaker makes. These concrete events are referred to as a speaker's **performance.**

This distinction has caused a lot of argument in current-day linguistics. Some sociologists regard it as an unreal distinction which ignores the importance of studying language in its social setting. They complain that many of today's grammars are based on unjustified assumptions concerning a speaker's competence (rather than on his actual utterances).

But the division is a useful one, if not carried to extremes. Ideally, the two approaches should complement one another. Any statements concerning a speaker's competence must ultimately be derived from data collected while studying his performance.

In fact, the distinction is one of long standing. De Saussure distinguished two concepts very similar to competence and performance, **langue** and **parole.**

By **langue,** de Saussure meant the shared communication system which all speakers have in common and which is automatically imposed on every child born into a community. By contrast, he regarded **parole** as referring to actual utterances by individuals.

De Saussure's *langue/parole* distinction closely resembles Chomsky's competence/performance dichotomy. The main difference is that de Saussure stressed the sociological implications of *langue*, while Chomsky stresses the psychological implications of competence.

These distinctions are also parallel to a distinction made between **code** and **message** in communications engineering. A **code** is the pre-arranged signalling system. A **message** is an actual message sent using that system.

Expression and Content

A language can be regarded as having two **planes,** expression and content.

On the **expression** plane, linguistics deals with the **form** or shape of linguistic elements without necessarily taking their meaning into account. From the point of view of form, 'Colourless green ideas sleep furiously' (a nonsense sentence made up by Chomsky) is a well-formed utterance.

The **content** plane deals with semantics, the study of **meaning.**

The study of form is less complex than the study of meaning. So the expression plane of a language is usually analysed before the content plane.

Levels of Analysis

On the expression plane, language can be split up into at least two layers or **levels.** Sounds are studied on one level, the elements formed by combinations of sounds on another.

As we have seen, every language possesses a stock of basic sound units or phonemes. The study of these units is known as **phonology.** A phoneme is meaningless by itself, but groups of phonemes form larger, meaningful units. These larger units are morphemes. The study of morphemes and the way they combine together into words is **morphology.**

Words can be combined together to form phrases and sentences. The study of this process is **syntax.**

Morphology and syntax together make up the level of **grammar.**

LEVELS OF ANALYSIS

PHONOLOGY	
MORPHOLOGY SYNTAX	} GRAMMAR

Exactly how many levels there are is disputed. Some people propose as many as five. Others say that rigid attempts to divide language into levels is misleading.

But there is no doubt that a preliminary sorting out into at least two levels is useful, providing one realises that the levels interact. The idea only becomes harmful when the different levels are treated as separate, water-tight compartments.

Hierarchical Structure

The level of phonology is relatively straightforward.

But on the level of grammar there are several types of unit: morphemes, words, phrases and sentences.

These form a **hierarchical structure,** in which smaller units combine to form successively larger units.

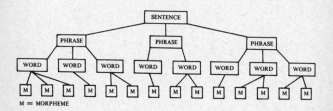

M = MORPHEME

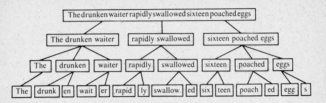

Where Should a Linguist Begin?

In analysing a language, linguists are faced with a problem—where should they begin?

Should they start with a largish chunk, such as a sentence, and then gradually break it down into smaller segments? Or should they start with the level of phonology?

There is no right or wrong way. Both methods are equally valid. This book begins by analysing sounds.

QUESTIONS

1. Distinguish between **synchronic** and **diachronic** approaches to language analysis.
2. Distinguish between **plane** and **level**.
3. Distinguish between **form** and **content**.
4. Explain the difference between **competence** and **performance**.
5. What is meant by **hierarchical structure**?

CHAPTER 5

Analysing Sounds

There was a young man of Dunlaoghaire,
Who propounded an interesting theoghaire,
*   That the language of Erse*
*   Has a shortage of verse*
As the spelling makes poets so weoghaire.

J. B. Searle

In a large number of languages, the conventional written forms provide little guide to the pronunciation. English, for example, has the words *tough*, *though*, *through*, *plough*. In each case, the letters *-ough* are pronounced differently. As de Saussure pointed out, 'Written forms obscure our view of language. They are not so much a garment as a disguise.'

As linguistics is concerned primarily with the **spoken** word (see Chapter 1), the first problem is to decide how to represent the flow of speech.

There are various systems of notation in which one symbol represents one sound. Perhaps the best known of these is the **International Phonetic Alphabet** (I.P.A.).

Many I.P.A. symbols are borrowed from the conventional written alphabet:

e.g. [b] as in *b*ird
    [d] as in *d*og.

Note that symbols representing sounds are put into square brackets.

Other symbols are variations of alphabet letters:

e.g. [ɒ] (upside down *a*) as in h*o*t,

or combinations of letters:

e.g. [ŋ] as in ba*ng*.

Sometimes obsolete letters are used:

e.g. [ʃ] as in di*sh*.

Other symbols are from the Greek alphabet:

e.g. [θ] as in *th*in,

and a few symbols are new inventions:

e.g. [ɬ] Welsh *ll* as in *Ll*ane*ll*y.

Sometimes accent marks or **diacritics** are added to the symbols. For example, two dots indicate length:

e.g. [uː] (long *u*) as in b*oo*t.

[ˌ] underneath a consonant indicates that it should be pronounced as a syllable:

e.g. [m̩] as in bott*om*
[n̩] as in butt*on*.

By such means, the I.P.A. has built up a store of symbols which can, in theory, represent any sound in any language.

Further information on phonetics is found in the Appendix, with a list of all the phonetic symbols found in this book. But, as phonetic symbols make a text more difficult to read, this book uses the conventional written letters wherever possible.

Writing Down an Unwritten Language

If a linguist wishes to write a grammar of an unwritten language, his first task is to find a suitable **informant**— a reliable native speaker from whom he can gather information.

In the early sessions, he asks the informant to name everyday objects, such as *nose, mouth, house, tree.* He transfers the sounds he hears into I.P.A. symbols—i.e. he makes a **phonetic transcription.**

This transcription will be as detailed or **narrow** as possible. Even sneezes and hiccups should be recorded in case they are relevant. In Zulu, for example, there are sounds known as **clicks** which an English speaker might well overlook. They are totally unlike any English speech sounds. The nearest equivalents are the clicking *gee-up* sound which people make to horses and the *tut-tut* click of disapproval.

Some sounds, such as *m* and *n*, occur in nearly all languages. Others, such as *th* in *th*ink and French *r*, occur only occasionally.

At first, the linguist may make a large number of mistakes. His native language is likely to influence him to a considerable extent.

An Englishman does not normally notice that the *p* in *p*ot is pronounced quite differently from the *p* in s*p*ot. Or that the sound at the beginning of *c*at is different from the sound at the beginning of *k*itten. Or that the *l* at the beginning of *l*eaf is different from the *l* in mi*l*k. He has been trained to ignore these distinctions, which may be vital in other languages.

As time goes on, he will transcribe more and more accurately. When he has collected a sufficiently large body of data, he can begin to disentangle the significant sounds or **phonemes** of the language.

Phonemes

The number of phonetic symbols used in a narrow transcription of a language may go into hundreds. But the number of phonemes will be much smaller.

The average number is around thirty-five. British

English has forty-four (or forty-five in some people's speech). Hawaian has thirteen, according to some reports, and one of the languages of the northern Caucasus has eighty-nine. These extremes are unusual, and the information may be unreliable.

A phoneme is a **minimum significant sound unit**—the smallest unit of sound which can bring about a change of meaning.

Phonemes can be identified by finding pairs of words with different meanings which differ by the smallest amount possible:

> e.g. *p*it and *b*it
> *r*ock and *l*ock
> pi*t* and pi*n*.

Such pairs of words are known as **minimal pairs.**

The contrasting sounds in a minimal pair will be separate phonemes:

> e.g. /p/ and /b/ in *p*it and *b*it
> /r/ and /l/ in *r*ock and *l*ock
> /t/ and /n/ in pi*t* and pi*n*.

Note that phonemes are put into slashed brackets.

The Phonemes of English

The phonemes of English can be divided into two types: **consonant-type** sounds and **vowel-type** sounds. Further phonetic information about these two types can be found in the Appendix.

Note that some of the vowels are relatively **pure** or unchanging vowels, as in b*i*t, b*e*t, b*a*t, b*u*t. And that others are **diphthongs** or gliding vowels, in which the voice glides from one vowel to another, as in b*oa*t, b*i*te, b*ai*t.

CONSONANT-TYPE	VOWEL-TYPE
/p/ as in *p*ill	/æ/ as in p*a*t
/b/ as in *b*ill	/ɑː/ as in p*ar*t
/t/ as in *t*in	/e/ as in p*e*t
/d/ as in *d*in	/ɪ/ as in p*i*t
/k/ as in *c*ot	/iː/ as in p*ea*t
/g/ as in *g*ot	/ɒ/ as in p*o*t
/m/ as in *m*eat	/ɔː/ as in p*or*t
/n/ as in *n*eat	/ʊ/ as in p*u*t
/ŋ/ as in si*ng*	/uː/ as in b*oo*t
/l/ as in *l*ake	/ʌ/ as in b*u*t
/r/ as in *r*ake	/ɜː/ as in b*ir*d
/f/ as in *f*ast	/ə/ as in *a*go
/v/ as in *v*ast	/eɪ/ as in b*ay*
/θ/ as in *th*in	/aɪ/ as in b*uy*
/ð/ as in *th*en	/ɔɪ/ as in b*oy*
/s/ as in *s*ink	/aʊ/ as in b*ou*t
/z/ as in *z*inc	/əʊ/ as in b*oa*t
/ʃ/ as in *sh*ip	/ɪə/ as in b*eer*
/ʒ/ as in bei*g*e	/ɛə/ as in b*are*
/h/ as in *h*at	/ʊə/ as in b*oor*
/ts/ as in *ch*in	
/dʒ/ as in *g*in	
/w/ as in *w*et	
/j/ as in *y*et	

Allophones

There is considerable variation in the pronunciation of phonemes. Variants of phonemes are known as **allophones.**

No two sounds can ever be uttered exactly the same, no matter how hard a speaker tries to repeat himself. These slight differences normally pass unnoticed, but they are always there.

Some differences are more obvious than others, as in

the pronunciation of /r/ in British English. Sometimes a speaker may roll the *r* in *rock*, at other times he may not. But different pronunciations of /r/ do not affect the meaning in any way. So these differing types of /r/ are said to be allophones of /r/ in **free variation.**

Occasionally, free variation can cause complications. An Englishman might not realise that Japanese [l] and [r] are in free variation, and are allophones of the same phoneme. Such overdifferentiation can lead to a faulty phonemic analysis.

Complementary Distribution

Sometimes an allophone occurs in a fixed place in a word. The English phoneme /l/, for example, has one form at the beginning of a word and another form at the end. In a word such as *lip*, the first consonant is a 'clear' *l*, pronounced by placing the tip of the tongue just behind the teeth and keeping the back of the tongue fairly low. In *pill*, the tongue tip is in the same place, but the back of the tongue is raised, resulting in a 'dark' *l*. These variants of /l/ are said to be in **complementary distribution:** each allophone occurs in its own predictable place in a word.

Another example of complementary distribution is seen in the English phoneme /p/. When *p* occurs at the beginning of a word, it is pronounced with aspiration (a puff of breath). After *s*, this puff of breath disappears. This can be tested by holding a sheet of paper in front of the mouth and saying the words *spot*, *spill*, *pot*, *pill*. In the case of *spot* and *spill*, the paper remains motionless. But when *pot* and *pill* are pronounced, the accompanying puff of breath makes the paper billow out.

Phonemic Patterning

Phonemes are never a haphazard collection of isolated elements. They always follow a definite pattern.

This pattern differs from language to language. It is to a large extent unconscious and appears to be one of the means by which human memory is able to store a large number of items.

In English, for example, many consonant phonemes are unconsciously paired together: /p/ is paired with /b/, /t/ is paired with /d/, /k/ is paired with /g/ and so on.

In addition, /p/ and /t/ and /k/ behave in a very similar way to one another. They each have an aspirated form which occurs at the beginning of a word, as in *pill*, *till*, *kill*, and an unaspirated form after /s/, as in *spill*, *still*, *skill*.

This patterning is particularly important in sound change (see Chapter 11).

Syllabic Structure

A different kind of sound patterning occurs within syllables.

Each language has its own characteristic **syllabic structure** which all words follow (except for occasional loan words). The rules for patterning within the syllable are strict and repetitive.

In English, for example, a word which begins with three consonant-type phonemes always obeys three strict rules:

1. The first phoneme must be /s/.
2. The second phoneme must be /p/ or /t/ or /k/.
3. The third phoneme must be /l/ or /r/ or /w/.

The result is that all words beginning with three consonants are words such as *spring*, *string*, *squeal* and *splendid*. We never find words such as *bdling*, *sgteal* or *wbtendid*.

Non-segmental Phonemes

Most phonemes consist of chunks or segments of sound,

such as /b/ or /t/ or /e/. These are known as **segmental** phonemes.

For an English speaking linguist, a particularly tricky problem is presented by a language such as Chinese which has **non-segmental** phonemes.

In North Mandarin Chinese, there are numerous examples of words which are distinguished by differences in tone, as in the following minimal pairs:

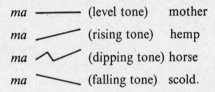

Sometimes such phonemic distinctions are accidentally ignored by European linguists and the resulting analysis is useless.

Tone languages may seem unnecessarily complex to Europeans. But they have one advantageous by-product. The tones and rhythms of speech can be imitated by instruments other than the human voice, and so (in primitive societies) the possibilities of communication are greater.

This is how African 'talking drums' work. The drum beats are a direct copy of the tones and rhythms of the language, and convey messages to villages for miles around.

Current Trends in Phonology

From one viewpoint, phonemes can be regarded as individual units which must be kept separate from one another.

But from a phonetic point of view, phonemes overlap to

a considerable extent. Each phoneme shares phonetic features with some others.

/p/ and /b/ and /m/, for example, each have a component (or feature) of **labiality** (they are all pronounced with the lips).

/m/ and /n/ both have a component of **nasality** (air is expelled through the nose as the sound is uttered).

This observation has led to an interesting development: the attempt to split phonemes into their component parts.

This type of analysis is known as **distinctive feature** analysis, since linguists are concerned with isolating those features which distinguish one phoneme from another.

It has been suggested that there are a fixed number of components which form a basic stockpile from which every language picks. Each language selects phonetic features from this common pool and combines them in different ways.

If this is so, it sheds a very interesting light on language universals, a subject of great interest in linguistics today.

QUESTIONS

1. What is a **phoneme?**
2. What is a **minimal pair?**
3. How many phonemes are there in British English?
4. What is an **allophone?**
5. Distinguish between **free variation** and **complementary distribution.**
6. What are **non-segmental** phonemes?

CHAPTER 6

Morphemes and Words

The smallest unit which has a grammatical function and an independent meaning is the **morpheme.**

Morphemes vary in size. Neither syllables nor length is any guide to their identification. The essential criterion is that a morpheme cannot be cut up into smaller grammatical segments.

The following sentence has eleven morphemes:

The	sleep	walk	ing	albatross	chant	ed	a	dream	y	lullaby.
1	2	3	4	5	6	7	8	9	10	11

The, *albatross*, *a*, *lullaby* are all single morphemes because none of them can be grammatically split up further. *Chanted* and *dreamy* are two-morpheme words. *Sleepwalking* is a three-morpheme word.

Morphemes are usually put into curly brackets:

{the} {sleep} {walk} {-ing} {albatross}

There are many more morphemes than phonemes in a language. Around 100 000 has been suggested as a reasonable figure for an educated man.

This vast number means that morphemes do not form a single, coherent pattern. There are many different types.

A basic distinction is that between **bound** and **free** morphemes.

Free morphemes can occur by themselves as independent words, such as *sleep*, *walk*, *albatross*, *chant*, *dream*, *lullaby*.

Bound morphemes can only occur attached to other morphemes, as *-ing*, *-ed*, *-y*.

Inflection and Derivation

Another important distinction is that between bound morphemes which are **inflectional** and those which are **derivational**.

Inflection changes the form of a word in order to express its relationship to other words in the sentence:

e.g. *cat* *cat*-**s**
  play *play*-**ed**
  sing *sing*-**ing**

Derivation changes an existing word into a new word:

e.g. *kind* *kind*-**ness**
  merry *merri*-**ly**
  obscene *obscen*-**ity**

Recognition of Morphemes

A linguist identifies morphemes by comparing a wide variety of utterances.

He looks for utterances which are **partially the same**:

The	dinosaur	sniff-*ed*	arrogant-*ly*	and	plodd-*ed*	for-*wards*.
The	dinosaur	snort-*ed*	loud-*ly*	and	edg-*ed*	back-*wards*.

The partial similarity between *sniffed*, *snorted*, *plodded* and *edged* enables a linguist to isolate the segment *-ed*. And the partial similarity between *arrogantly* and *loudly*, and between *backwards* and *forwards* enables him to isolate *-ly* and *-wards*.

In Turkish, the similarity between *adamlar* 'men' and *kadınlar* 'women' enables one to identify a plural suffix—*lar*.

Not all morphemes are as easily segmentable as these

examples. But the identification of morphemes is done wholly by means of this one basic technique—the comparison of partially similar utterances.

Morphs and Allomorphs

Sometimes a morpheme has only one **morph,** or phonological form:

e.g.   loud   /laʊd/
-ly   /-lɪ/.

But frequently a morpheme has a number of variants known as **allomorphs.**

Allomorphs are not always easy to classify. Totally dissimilar forms may be allomorphs of the same morpheme. *Cats*, *dogs*, *horses*, *sheep*, *oxen*, *geese* all contain the English plural morpheme.

An allomorph is said to be **phonologically conditioned** when its form is dependent on the adjacent phonemes. It is **morphologically conditioned** when there is no phonological conditioning factor.

Phonological Conditioning

The English plural morpheme provides excellent examples of both phonologically and morphologically conditioned allomorphs.

The most frequent allomorph is /-z/ (as in *dogs*). For this reason, the plural morpheme is often referred to as {-z}. (Note that allomorphs are written phonemically in slashed brackets. As mentioned above, morphemes are indicated by curly brackets.)

/-z/ /-s/ /-ɪz/ are all phonologically conditioned allomorphs of the English plural morpheme:

/-z/ occurs after most voiced phonemes, as in *dogs*, *lambs*, *bees*. (For explanations of phonetic terms, see the Appendix.)

/-s/ occurs after most voiceless phonemes, as in *cats*, *giraffes*, *skunks*.

/-ɪz/ occurs mainly after sibilants, as in *horses*, *cheeses*, *dishes*.

$$dog + /-z/$$
$$cat + /-s/$$
$$horse + /-ɪz/$$

(Note that this is only a partial account of the conditioning of English plural {-z}. For a more complete account, see the books recommended in the Appendix.)

The study of the different phonemic shapes of allomorphs is halfway between phonology and morphology, and is sometimes referred to as **morphophonology** (occasionally abbreviated to **morphonology**).

Morphological Conditioning

Words such as *oxen*, *sheep*, *geese* present a problem. Although they function as plurals in the same way as *cats*, *dogs*, they are not marked as plurals in the same way. Such morphologically conditioned plurals are more difficult to identify and analyse.

Oxen, *sheep*, *geese* can be identified as grammatically equivalent to the *cats* and *dogs* type of plural because they fit into the same 'slot' in a sentence:

e.g. The — are making a lot of noise.

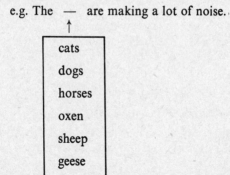

Oxen, *sheep* and *geese* can each be said to represent two morphemes:

> ox + plural
> sheep + plural
> goose + plural.

But only *oxen* is easily divisible into two:

> ox + /-ən/ (-*en*).

Sheep can be divided into two if a **zero suffix** is assumed. A 'zero suffix' is a convenient linguistic fiction which is most useful in cases of this type. It is normally written /ø/:

> sheep + /ø/.

There is no obvious way to analyse *geese*. Some linguists suggest that the plural vowel /iː/ in /giːs/ (*geese*) which replaces the /uː/ in /guːs/ (*goose*) should be regarded as a special type of morphemic element called a **replacive.** And they would analyse the plural as:

> /guːs/ + /iː/ ← (/uː/).

Here the formula /iː/ ← (/uː/) means '/iː/ replaces /uː/'.

But this is a rather strained explanation. It is possibly better to state simply that the form /giːs/ (*geese*) represents two morphemes,

> goose + plural

and that these two cannot be separated.

Note that a similar explanation is required for forms such as *went*, *took*, which represent

> go + past tense
> take + past tense.

Other Problems of Morpheme Division

Different problems of morpheme division are presented by words such as *cranberry* and *hamburger*.

Cranberry, along with words such as *raspberry*, represents the so-called 'cranberry morph' problem.

At first sight, such words appear to consist of two morphemes: *cran-berry*, *rasp-berry*. On second sight, it is difficult to justify *cran-* and *rasp-* as independent morphemes.

These elements occur only in these words, so splitting up the word seems unjustifiable. There is a word *cran* 'measure for fresh herrings, $37\frac{1}{2}$ gallons'. But this is in no way connected with *cran-* of *cranberry* and so does not count.

The linguist must make his own decision by choosing the solution which seems more economical and consistent.

Cranberry is, in general, analysed as two morphemes in order to bring it in line with words such as *blackberry*. *Cran-* is then regarded as a **unique morpheme** (i.e. a morpheme which occurs once only).

A similar problem is raised by the English *wh-* and *th-* words:

> *where* — *there*
> *when* — *then*
> *whither* — *thither*.

Should these be analysed as two morphemes, *wh- ere*, *th- ere* and so on?

Perhaps this would be a good solution if they were the only *wh-* words English possessed. The situation is complicated by the existence of *who*, *why*, which do not have *th-* correlates. Since *who*, *why* cannot be divided, it may be more satisfactory to keep *where*, *when*, *whither* as single morphemes also.

A different problem arises with words such as *hamburger*. This is obviously divisible into two morphemes. But where does the division come? Some people would suggest *hamburg-er*, remembering that *hamburger* was named after Hamburg, its town of origin. But on the basis of *cheeseburger*, *fishburger*, the division should obviously be *ham-burger*.

Nowadays, *-burger* seems to be treated as a suffix and is found increasingly in various type of rissole (*fishburger*, *kingburger*, etc.). So *ham-burger* is possibly a better solution. Most people have forgotten the German origin of these foods, and historical considerations should never be taken into account in a descriptive analysis.

Provisional Summary

A morpheme can be defined as the smallest grammatical and smallest meaningful unit.

Morphemes cover a wide variety of types. The most basic distinction is into bound and free morphemes. Another important distinction is that between inflectional and derivational bound morphemes.

A linguist identifies the morphemes in a language by comparing utterances which are partially alike.

He draws up a list of the allomorphs used to represent each morpheme. These allomorphs may be phonologically or morphologically conditioned.

Where the division into morphemes is unclear, he chooses the most economical or consistent solution.

Morphemes and Words

The number of morphemes per word varies from language to language—so does the way in which morphemes are combined.

In the nineteenth century, scholars tried to use such criteria for dividing languages into different types. They recognised at least *three* different morphological types.

An **isolating** (or analytical) language is one in which words frequently consist of one morpheme. This is often the case in English:

e.g. Will you please let the dog out now.

An **agglutinating** language (from the Latin word for 'glue together') is one in which words can be divided into morphemes without difficulty. Turkish is the best-known example. But agglutination is also used to a limited extent in English:

e.g. lov-ing-ly   faith-ful-ness.

A **fusional** (or inflecting) language is one such as Latin which fuses morphemes together in such a way that they are not easily recognisable as separate elements. As seen above, occasional examples of fusion occur in English:

e.g. *went* = *go* + past tense.

At one time it was thought that languages followed a fixed pattern of development. The first stage was an isolating one, the second stage agglutinating, the third inflecting. Greek and Latin were spoken of in sentimental terms as representing the highest and best of language types. Everything else was regarded as an aberration or a symptom of decline and decay. The fallacy of such a belief is pointed out vividly by the American Edward Sapir: 'A linguist that insists on talking about the Latin type of morphology as though it were necessarily the high-water mark of linguistic development is like the zoologist that sees in the organic world a huge conspiracy to evolve the race-horse or the Jersey cow'.

The other flaw in this type of classification is that no language is a 'pure' morphological type. A few languages fit into one category rather than another, but many appear to have mixed morphological processes.

Words

The **word** appears to be a universal concept. Even in primitive cultures, informants seem able to identify words. But no one has yet proposed a satisfactory definition.

The best known definition is that proposed by the American linguist Bloomfield, who defined a word as a **minimum free form,** i.e. the smallest form that can occur by itself.

This definition works best for written English. Unfortunately, it does not apply to all languages, nor to all types of word. The reason is that the word *word* covers a variety of different concepts.

The most obvious type of word is the written (or **orthographical**) word. In English, this is simple to define, since we conventionally leave a space either side of it. Occasionally, a writer is uncertain whether a form is one word or two, as with *alright* or *all right*. But this is a minor problem. (Note that not all writing systems leave spaces between words: Devanāgarī, the script used for the old Indian language Sanskrit, joins all the words together.)

The spoken equivalent of the orthographical word is the **phonological** word. The phonological word /hɪt/, for example, corresponds to the written word *hit:*

> *hit*   orthographical
> /hɪt/   phonological.

But phonological and orthographical words often represent more than one **grammatical** word.

Orthographical *hit* represents both the noun *hit*, the present and past tenses of the verb, and the past participle—four different grammatical words:

1. The play was a big *hit*.
2. Why do you always *hit* your baby brother?

3. He *hit* me!

4. He was *hit* by a bullet.

A **lexical** word is best described as a 'dictionary entry'. It is the abstract entity which is felt to underlie the various inflected forms. *Howl, howling, howled* are different orthographical and grammatical words, but only one lexical word. In a dictionary, they would all come under the entry *howl*:

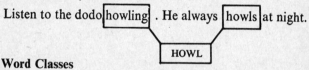

Listen to the dodo howling . He always howls at night.

HOWL

Word Classes

Every language has a number of different types of grammatical word or **word classes** (traditionally known as parts of speech). Some of them, such as the classes of noun and verb, may be universal.

In order to classify words into classes, the test of substitution is used. A linguist draws up a list of possible substitutes for each 'slot' in a sentence:

SLOT 1	SLOT 2	SLOT 3	SLOT 4	SLOT 5	SLOT 6
The	lonely	dinosaur	swallowed	a	fly.
A	greedy	kangaroo	ate	that	bird.
This	stupid	bird	followed	this	dinosaur.
That	small	fly	chased	that	kangaroo.

SLOT 1 = SLOT 5   SLOT 3 = SLOT 6

The same words are found in slots 1 and 5, so these must belong to the same word class. The same applies to slots 3 and 6.

This type of substitution test is basic to all levels of linguistics as a means of discovering whether items are similar or dissimilar.

Note, however, that such substitution tests are rarely as straightforward as the example given above. In English, a pronoun, such as *I, you, he* might be found covering slots 1–3:

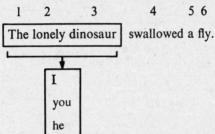

This type of problem is usually considered under the heading of syntax, which will be discussed in the following chapter.

Note also that the eight parts of speech found in many English text books are based to a large extent on ancient Greek grammars, and cannot be justified linguistically. The term 'adverb', for example, includes a rag-bag selection of words which fit into quite different 'slots' in the sentence:

e.g. He ran quickly,
but not *He ran very.[1]

Yet both *very* and *quickly* are usually classified as adverbs.

The number of word classes varies from language to language. The smallest number reported so far is two, in Nootka, an American-Indian language—though more recent studies suggest this may be an oversimplification.

This raises a fascinating question. Is it possible to reduce a large number of word classes down to one or

[1] An asterisk denotes a sentence that is grammatically unacceptable.

two basic ones? For example, is the distinction normally found in English between an adjective and a verb merely superficial?

In the sentences

> John is *running*
> John is *good*

both *running* and *good* seem to have the same relationship to *John*—so perhaps this is so. This type of question is under heated discussion in linguistics at the moment.

Open and Closed Word Classes

Word classes fall into two main groups, **open** and **closed.**

Open classes are those which have an indefinite number of words in them, such as nouns and verbs. A noun is an open word class because people can make up any number of new nouns without affecting the structure of the language.

Closed word classes are those which have a fixed number of members, such as pronouns. English, for example, has the personal pronouns *I*, *you*, *he*, *she*, *it*, *we*, *they*, (*thou*).

But words do not divide neatly into one or the other of these two classes. They are on a gradual slope, leading from closed to open. The class of preposition, for example, is more open than that of pronoun, but less open than that of noun. A new preposition can occasionally be introduced, as in the sentence 'He fell overside the boat'.

OPEN ←		WORD CLASSES			→ CLOSED
NOUN	ADJECTIVE	VERB	PREPOSITION	CONJUNCTION	PRONOUN
table	good	sleep	into	and	I,
tree	happy	jump	onto	or	you
moon	blue	swim	up	but	he, she, it
chair	white	sit	down	since	we
horse	true	love			they
cow	sad	hate			

Full and Empty Words

Another related distinction is that between **full** and **empty** words.

Full words have some kind of intrinsic meaning. They refer to objects, actions and qualities that can be identified in the external world, such as *table*, *tree*, *jump*, *sleep*, *blue*. Such words are said to have **lexical meaning.**

Empty words have little or no intrinsic meaning. They exist because of their grammatical function in the sentence. For example, *and* is used for joining items, *or* indicates alternatives, *of* sometimes indicates possession. These words have **grammatical meaning.**

In general, open word classes contain words with lexical meaning (full words), sloping gradually down towards closed classes containing words with grammatical meaning (empty words).

Because there are no clear-cut lines between these two types of word, the relationship between grammar and meaning is complex.

QUESTIONS

1. Distinguish between **phonologically** and **morphologically** conditioned allomorphs.
2. What is a **zero morph?**
3. What is the **'cranberry morph'** problem?
4. Distinguish between **inflection** and **derivation.**
5. Explain the connection between **full** words and **open** word classes.

CHAPTER 7

Syntax

The word **syntax** is derived from a Greek word meaning 'arrangement'. This explains well what syntax entails. It studies the ways in which words are arranged together in order to make larger units.

The sentence is normally taken as the largest unit amenable to useful linguistic analysis. So a syntactic analysis is concerned with sentences and the constituents of sentences.

Constituent is a useful blanket word, used to refer to a component part of a sentence. For this reason, syntactic analysis of a sentence is sometimes referred to as **constituent analysis.**

Sentences are **strings** of words (i.e. they are composed of words strung together). But these strings are not random. 'Policeman park a by near stopped the was he' is unstructured, ungrammatical and meaningless. 'He was stopped by a policeman near the park' is structured, grammatical and meaningful. So a sentence is a **structured string.**

Linguists are interested in two aspects of this structuring. Firstly, they are interested in the patterns underlying the sentence and its constituents. Secondly, they are interested in the syntactic devices used to link the constituents together, and the ways in which the various parts relate to one another.

Basic Sentence Types

Every language has a limited number of basic sentence

types to which most sentences can be reduced. A fundamental technique in syntactic analysis is to reduce a sentence to one of these basic types by a process of successive substitution:

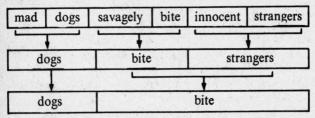

The substitutes progressively simplify the sentence, but do not alter the basic pattern in any way. Such substitution continues until the sentence cannot be reduced any further.

Tree Diagrams

The complex layering of a sentence can be represented most clearly by a **tree diagram**—so called because its branches resemble the branches of a tree. It is also known as a **phrase marker.**

In a tree diagram, a basic sentence type at the top branches out downwards in ever increasing complexity:

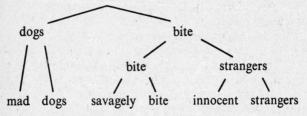

Bracketing and Labelling

The advantage of a tree diagram is that each join or **node** on the tree can be labelled, so that the whole construction becomes clearer.

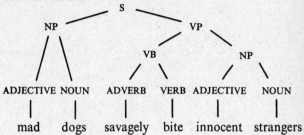

s—Sentence   NP—Noun Phrase   VP—Verb Phrase

The whole process of syntactic analysis is sometimes referred to as **bracketing and labelling.** Closely related constituents are bracketed together and then given the appropriate syntactic label.

For example, in the diagrams above, ADJECTIVE + NOUN are bracketed together under the label NP (NOUN PHRASE).

The bracketing and labelling of successive layers of constituents is common to all syntactic analyses—though linguists differ as to how the constituents should be bracketed. They also disagree about the number of layers into which a sentence can usefully be analysed.

Rewrite Rules

An alternative way of expressing the information found on a tree diagram is by means of **rewrite rules.**

A rewrite rule is a replacement rule, in which the symbol to the left of an arrow is replaced by an expanded form written to the right of the arrow:

e.g. S $\Rightarrow$ NP + VP

means 'Replace the symbol S by NP + VP'.

On a tree diagram, this would appear as:

The sentence 'Mad dogs savagely bite innocent strangers' could be rewritten as follows:

$$\text{S} \rightarrow \text{NP} + \text{VP}$$
$$\text{VP} \rightarrow \text{VB} + \text{NP}$$
$$\text{NP} \rightarrow \text{ADJECTIVE} + \text{NOUN}$$
$$\text{VB} \rightarrow \text{ADVERB} + \text{VERB}$$
$$\text{ADJECTIVE} \rightarrow \text{mad, innocent}$$
$$\text{NOUN} \rightarrow \text{dogs, strangers}$$
$$\text{ADVERB} \rightarrow \text{savagely}$$
$$\text{VERB} \rightarrow \text{bite}$$

The great advantage of rewrite rules is that they are perfectly **explicit.** They do not leave anything to the imagination. By following them, you could produce a perfect English sentence even if you did not know any English, since the rules are applied mechanically step-by-step, one symbol at a time.

Discontinuous Constituents

Constituent analysis is rarely as simple as the example given. Usually one or more of a number of difficulties crops up.

A common problem in English is the occurrence of **discontinuous constituents:**

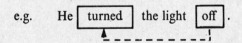

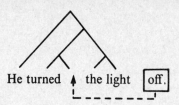

He turned ▲ the light │ off │.

Embedding and Conjoining

English constituent analysis is further complicated by
frequent **embedding.** A large number of sentences have
another sentence-like construction embedded inside them:

> e.g. The rumour that the dinosaur had escaped worried
> the public.

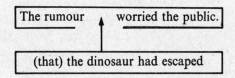

In theory, a sentence can have an indefinite number of
sentences embedded in it. In 'The fact that the rumour that
the dinosaur had escaped worried the public is not surprising', the simple sentence has two others embedded
in it:

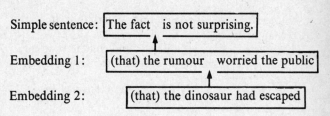

Another example of embedding is the old nursery rhyme:

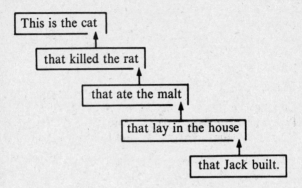

Conjoining also causes difficulties. This occurs when elements are added (or joined) to other similar elements:

e.g.   Do you want gin or whisky or vodka or martini ?

John and Mary   and Peter went to the cinema.

Archibald played tennis,

and Douglas played cricket,

but Peter went fishing.

Both embedding and conjoining illustrate an important property of language—that of **recursion.**

Recursion is the possibility of indefinitely re-applying the same rule of grammar, so that a sentence may be (in theory) infinitely long.

Any grammar must take this important facet of language into account.

Deep and Surface Structure

Perhaps the greatest weakness of straightforward constituent analysis is its inability to distinguish between **deep** and **surface** structures.

In a language, it often happens that two sentences are superficially alike, but basically quite different:

e.g. The octopus was anxious to eat.

The octopus was delicious to eat.

These sentences both follow the same grammatical pattern, and have the same phrase marker:

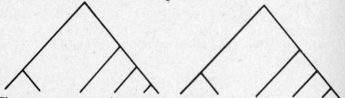

The octopus was anxious to eat. The octopus was delicious to eat.

But in the first sentence, the octopus is doing the eating. In the second, the octopus is being eaten. The difference is shown clearly if the sentences are switched around:

Eating the octopus was delicious.

*Eating the octopus was anxious.

In such cases, linguists say that the sentences have a similar **surface** structure, but differing **deep** structures.

This distinction is of extreme importance in transformational grammar (see Chapter 8).

Syntactic Devices

In the sentence:

The large spider terrified Aunt Matilda,

how do we know that it is *Aunt Matilda* who was frightened, not the spider? How do we know that *large* refers to the spider, not to Aunt Matilda?

Such matters are made clear by the use of syntactic devices. These vary from language to language, but similar devices recur. Most languages have one or two favourite devices and several other subsidiary ones.

Word order is the device used above all in English:

> The large spider terrified Aunt Matilda.
> Aunt Matilda terrified the large spider.

The words themselves in these two sentences are identical. It is word order only which indicates who frightened whom.

Another device found in English is the use of **function words.** These are the so-called 'empty words', such as *of*, *by*, which exist solely to indicate grammatical relationships:

> He was hit *by* a car.
> The Queen *of* Sheba.

In a language such as Latin, **concord** (or **agreement**) is the favourite device:

> Magna aranea perterruit Matildam amitam.
> (The large spider terrified Aunt Matilda.)

Here it is the concord between *magna* and *aranea* which indicates that the two words go together. Word order is irrelevant. The sentence would still mean the same if the words were arranged quite differently:

> Magna Matildam perterruit amitam aranea.
> (large—Matilda—terrified—aunt—spider)

Concord occurs occasionally in English. In *he swims* there is concord between *he* and the morpheme -*s* at the end of *swims*.

Sometimes syntactic features can be indicated by intonation. This is a possible way of distinguishing between questions and statements in English. *He's going home* (statement) may be distinguished from *He's going home?* (question) purely by intonation, as the voice often rises at the end of a question.

It is sometimes suggested that morphology and syntax counterbalance one another: that a language with a complex morphology tends to have a relatively simple syntax, and that a language which is morphologically fairly simple is likely to be syntactically complex. But this is still unproved.

'Subject' of a Sentence?

One of the questions much discussed at the moment is that of the relationships between the different parts of a sentence.

In traditional grammar, this type of discussion did not arise. It was assumed automatically that a sentence could be divided into subject and predicate. The subject was a noun (or noun phrase) and the predicate contained further information concerning that noun:

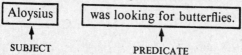

| Aloysius | was looking for butterflies. |

SUBJECT   PREDICATE

But, on closer inspection, various inconsistencies show themselves with regard to the so-called **subject**.

In an inflected language, such as Latin, the subject of a sentence is normally the grammatical subject, identified by the use of the nominative case:

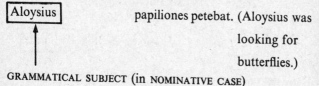

Aloysius papiliones petebat. (Aloysius was looking for butterflies.)

GRAMMATICAL SUBJECT (in NOMINATIVE CASE)

But in English, where there is not normally a case-ending to mark the grammatical subject, it can get confused with the subject of conversation—though this happens more frequently in literary language and poetry than in everyday English:

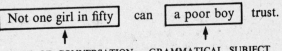

Not one girl in fifty | can | a poor boy | trust.

SUBJECT OF CONVERSATION   GRAMMATICAL SUBJECT

To avoid confusion, linguists tend to speak of **topic** and **comment** in such circumstances. You bring up a topic of conversation and then make a comment about it:

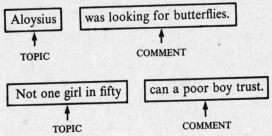

Aloysius | was looking for butterflies.

TOPIC   COMMENT

Not one girl in fifty | can a poor boy trust.

TOPIC   COMMENT

A further difficulty is the tendency to confuse the so-called subject of a sentence with the **actor** or **agent** (the doer of the action):

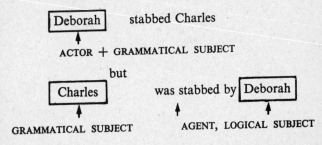

Deborah | stabbed Charles

ACTOR + GRAMMATICAL SUBJECT

but

Charles | was stabbed by | Deborah

GRAMMATICAL SUBJECT   AGENT, LOGICAL SUBJECT

So the word **subject** should sometimes be avoided and replaced by a less ambiguous term such as topic or actor. This brief discussion only scratches the surface of the immensely complex nature of this type of problem.

'Object' of a Sentence?

The so-called object of a sentence is also a maze of complexity.

Traditionally, verbs are divided into two types, **transitive** and **intransitive.** Those which take an object are **transitive** (from the Latin verb 'to cross over'; the action of the verb is presumed to cross over to the object):

e.g. Gregory *killed* an octopus.

Verbs without an object are **intransitive:**

e.g. The octopus *died.*

But this simple picture is complicated by a number of factors.

Firstly, the word **object** covers at least two different types of object, an ordinary object and an **object of result:**

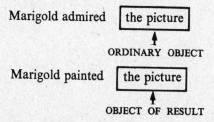

Marigold admired ┌ the picture ┐
                 ORDINARY OBJECT

Marigold painted ┌ the picture ┐
                 OBJECT OF RESULT

In the first sentence, the object already existed before Mary admired it. In the second, the picture is the direct result of Mary's action.

Another complexity is the existence of a number of transitive verbs where the object is 'understood', or **deleted** in linguistic terminology. This gives them the false impression of being intransitive:

> Alfred is eating (his dinner).
> Alfred is writing (a letter).

Linguists are currently attempting to unravel the deep structure behind these various surface structures.

QUESTIONS
1. What is meant by **bracketing and labelling?**
2. What is **recursion?**
3. Distinguish between **deep** and **surface** structure.
4. Name and illustrate three **syntactic devices** found in English.
5. Why does the word **subject** cause confusion in linguistics?

CHAPTER 8

Chomsky and Transformational Grammar

Noam Chomsky is, arguably, the most influential linguistic scholar of the century. Certainly he is the linguist whose reputation has spread furthest outside linguistics.

His book *Syntactic Structures* (1957) gained almost instant recognition as a work of immense importance. Yet Chomsky and transformational grammar have acquired a glamour and mystery out of all proportion to the basically simple (though undoubtedly brilliant) ideas put forward.

The pro-Chomsky fervour of the 1960s can be explained partly by historical reasons.

In the 1950s, linguistics was in the doldrums, particularly in America. The whole linguistics movement had become narrow and introverted. There had been no major change of direction in linguistics for more than twenty years (see Chapter 3). When Chomsky arrived on the scene, linguistics was ready for new ideas.

As noted in Chapter 3, Chomsky's contribution was twofold. Firstly, he questioned the goals towards which linguistic theory was oriented, and redefined the aims and functions of a 'grammar'. Secondly, he specified the form this new grammar should take—that of a transformational grammar.

The Goals of Linguistic Theory and the Concept of Grammar

Between 1933 and 1957, linguistics had set itself the task of perfecting 'discovery procedures': that is, finding a set of principles which would enable a linguist to 'discover' or extract a grammar from a mass of data collected from an informant. In order that such a grammar should be as 'scientific' as possible, it should ideally be written solely by studying the patterns found in a language without reference to meaning.

So, at this time, a grammar could be defined as a perfect, objective description of a language. And the ultimate goal of linguistics was to find rules which led to such grammars.

Chomsky suggested that this aim was both far too ambitious and far too limited in scope. It was too ambitious in that it was unrealistic to expect to be able to lay down foolproof rules for extracting a perfect grammar from a mass of data. It was too limited because such grammars had no predictive power. They catalogued what had happened, but did not predict what would happen.

He suggested that a grammar should be regarded, instead, as a theory or hypothesis about how a language worked. In the same way as a biochemist might formulate a hypothesis about how cells multiply and would then test this hypothesis against actual living cells, so a grammar should be a hypothesis about language formulated and tested in the same way.

If correctly formulated, such a grammar will be 'a device that generates all of the grammatical sequences [of a language] and none of the ungrammatical ones'.

The task of linguistics was to formulate such grammars and to work out principles by which they could be evaluated—so that, if a linguist was presented with two rival grammars, he could automatically identify the better of the two and reject the other.

Generative Grammar

Chomsky, then, insisted that a grammar must be **predictive.** It must generate **potential** grammatical sequences, as well as actual ones.

Chomsky also insisted that a grammar should be perfectly **explicit.** It should leave nothing to the imagination and should be formulated step-by-step in such a way that the generation of the sentences of a language should be a purely mechanical procedure. Even a person who did not know the language could generate sentences by following the step-by-step rules.

The **explicitness** and the **predictive** nature of such a grammar can be summed up in one word, the word **generative.**

The word **generative** is frequently misunderstood. It is often, wrongly, used synonymously with transformational.

But the two must be kept separate. Any type of grammar which is explicit and predictive is generative. But not all generative grammars are transformational.

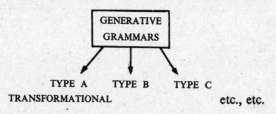

Transformational Grammar

Most languages have a number of constructions which are superficially different, but which their speakers

intuitively feel to be related at some 'deeper' level: that is, they have a similar **deep** structure, but different **surface** structures. (For the distinction between deep and surface structures, see also Chapter 7.)

   e.g. Alexander shot the elephant.
       Did Alexander shoot the elephant?
       The elephant was shot by Alexander.

In a transformational grammar (as it was first formulated), all such sentences were derived from one underlying 'kernel'.

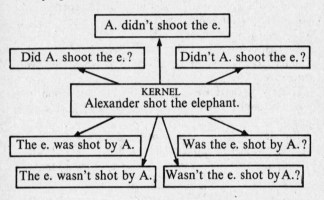

The underlying deep structure kernel was converted or **transformed** into the different surface structure realisations by processes known as **transformations.**

So a **transformational grammar** can be defined as a grammar which converts deep structures into surface structures by means of transformations.

On the one hand, transformations can relate different surface structures to the same deep structure kernel (as above). On the other hand, they can account for sentences which appear similar, but are intuitively felt to be different, such as 'John is eager to please' and John is easy to please'

These two sentences are derived from different deep structure kernels. 'John is eager to please' has a kernel similar to its surface structure. But 'John is easy to please' has a kernel more like 'It is easy to please John' The similarity results from a transformation which re-ordered the words of this kernel.[1]

Components of a Transformational Grammar (1957)

'There are three things in life you must never run after: a woman, a bus and a theory of transformational grammar—there will be another one along in a moment' remarked one well-known linguist.

Chomsky has modified many details in his grammar since the publication of *Syntactic Structures* (1957). A later version appeared in 1965, but modifications are still being made.

As there is no definitive version (nor does it look as if there is likely to be one), it is perhaps simplest to approach transformational grammar from its earliest formulation.

In *Syntactic Structures*, the grammar is viewed as being in three parts:

    (i) phrase structure (PS) component
    (ii) transformational (TFL) component
    (iii) morphophonemic (MPH) component.

It is conventionally depicted as a kind of machine in which a sentence is pictured as progressing through each of the components in turn, moving from deep to surface structure.

---

[1] More accurately, each of these sentences is formed from *two* under-lying kernels:
    (i) John is eager—John pleases.
    (ii) It is easy—someone pleases John.

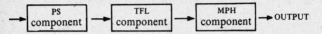

The **phrase structure** component generates the structure which underlies a kernel sentence by means of rewrite rules (for an explanation of rewrite rules, see Chapter 7).

So (in a much simplified version) we might get:

$$S \rightarrow NP + VP$$
$$VP \rightarrow V + NP$$
$$NP \rightarrow \begin{cases} \text{Proper } N \\ D + N \end{cases}$$
$$\text{Proper } N \rightarrow \text{Alexander}$$
$$D \rightarrow \text{the}$$
$$N \rightarrow \text{elephant}$$
$$V \rightarrow \text{shot}$$

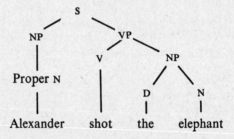

The **transformational** component contains rules which can alter the kernel in various ways. 'Alexander shot the elephant' could be transformed into 'The elephant was shot by Alexander' by means of a passive transformation. This would be a rule specifying that NP_1 (Alexander) must change places with NP_2 (the elephant); and that part of the verb *to be* and *by* must be inserted before V (shot) and NP_1 (Alexander) respectively.

Alternatively, 'Alexander shot the elephant' could have been transformed into a question or a negative.

Or the negative, question and passive transformations could have been applied in turn, resulting in 'Wasn't the elephant shot by Alexander?'.

The negative, question and passive transformations are all **optional,** and could have been omitted.

Other transformations are **obligatory,** such as the 'number' transformation, which deals with the agreement of a noun phrase with its verb. In 'The elephant was shot by Alexander' the number transformation specifies that a singular noun phrase (*the elephant*) must be followed by a singular verb (*was*).

Note also that transformations have to be applied in a definite order. The number transformation must be applied *after* the passive transformation. If the order of these two transformations was reversed, the verb would agree with the wrong noun phrase, resulting in ungrammatical strings such as:

> *The buns was eaten by the elephant.
> *The elephant were shot by the hunters.

The **morphophonemic** component converts the output of the transformational component into a phonemic transcription. So 'The elephant was shot by Alexander' would become:

/ði elɪfənt wəz ʃɒt baɪ æleksɑːndə/

This early form of transformational grammar shows the essential ideas behind Chomsky's writings, which are still best approached via *Syntactic Structures*.

In later versions, Chomsky's terminology (and views) changed. **Kernels, PS component, morphophonemic component, optional transformations** no longer occur as such.

No detailed account of the changes can be given—but a few noticeable differences are mentioned below.

Components of a Transformational Grammar (1965)

Chomsky 'Mark II' grammar (as it is sometimes called) is propounded in *Aspects of the Theory of Syntax* (1965).

This is a more difficult book to read, partly because it assumes a knowledge of the extensive discussions of transformational grammar which took place between 1957 and 1965.

The most notable difference is the inclusion of a totally new **semantic** component to deal with meaning. This is attached at deep structure level.

The phrase structure component is modified and renamed the **base** component. And the morphophonemic component is renamed the **phonological** component.

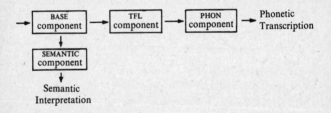

Another significant difference is the abolishing of optional transformations. Negatives, questions and passives are no longer introduced optionally at the stage of the transformational component, but are partially incorporated into the base.

Instead of generating a kernel only, the base component includes deep structure 'notes' on the various transformations to take place:

e.g. <u>DEEP STRUCTURE</u>

(simplified)

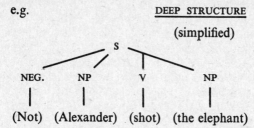

| NEG. | NP | V | NP |
| (Not) | (Alexander) | (shot) | (the elephant) |

When such a note exists, it is the transformational component which obligatorily converts the string into its surface structure realisation.

The **phonological** component is envisaged as containing a stock of universally valid phonetic features (components of phonemes, see Chapter 5). Each language selects and combines these features in different ways in order to provide a phonetic transcription for the output of the transformational component.

This account of transformational grammar is overbrief and oversimplified. See the suggestions for further reading in the Appendix for books which give a fuller account and which can act as stepping stones to the writings of Chomsky.

Ideas Arising from Chomsky

An interesting theory supported by some transformationalists is that the deep structure of all languages may be similar. Perhaps languages differ only in their choice of transformation.

If this were so, it would have exciting repercussions.

In translation (or language learning), a translator would only have to know which transformations were used by each language. If he were translating from English to French, for example, he would strip away the surface structure of English and be left with the universal deep structure. He could then apply the transformations used by French and the task would be done.

Another interesting possibility is that children may have an innate knowledge of deep structure. Perhaps all they have to learn in order to speak are the specific transformations used by their own particular language.

But such suggestions are highly controversial, and as yet no fully satisfactory proposals for universal deep structures have been made.

One particularly tricky question is the integration of meaning and syntax in deep structure. Many linguists are coming to the conclusion that meaning should not be 'tacked on' to deep structure syntax, but may even underlie it at a still 'deeper' level. Others are proposing that deep structure syntax may itself be far more abstract and less tangible than is suggested in Chomsky's writings.

Such questions are likely to take up the attention of linguists for many years to come.

QUESTIONS

1. What, according to Chomsky, are the goals of linguistic theory?
2. What is a **generative** grammar?
3. What is a **transformational** grammar?
4. What is a **kernel?**
5. What components are required in a transformational grammar in:

   (a) 1957 version?
   (b) 1965 version?

CHAPTER 9

Meaning

The study of meaning is normally referred to as **semantics,** from the Greek noun *sema* 'sign, signal' and the verb *semaino* 'signal, mean'.

When we talk about meaning, we are talking about the ability of human beings to understand each other when they speak. This ability is to some extent connected with grammar. No one could understand:

hat one the the but red blue on bought tried Miranda

while

Miranda tried on the red hat but bought the blue one

causes no difficulties.

Yet there are numerous sentences which are perfectly grammatical but meaningless. The most famous example is:

Colourless green ideas sleep furiously.

Other similar examples are:

The pregnant bachelor gave birth to six rabbits tomorrow.
The chair sneezed apologetically.

So a linguist would like to find out why an English speaker automatically accepts and understands a sentence such as:

Englebert admired the rainbow

and rejects as meaningless

> Colourless green ideas sleep furiously

even though he might never have heard either sentence before.

Connected with this automatic acceptance or rejection of sentences are various other related abilities.

First, there is the ability to paraphrase. An Englishman would automatically link up the following sentences by realising that one is a paraphrase of the other:

> Show me the way to go home.
> Indicate to me the route to my habitual abode.

Secondly, there is the ability to detect ambiguities, as in:

> Visiting great-aunts can be a nuisance.

Thirdly, there is the ability to resolve these ambiguities by reference to the surrounding context:

> Visiting great-aunts can be a nuisance: I wish we didn't have to go.

A linguist would like to find out how a man is able to paraphrase and detect ambiguities, and why the surrounding words sometimes force him to choose one interpretation rather than another.

Meaning and the Outside World

'Meaning' is double-faced. The meaning of a word such as *tree* must be considered in two ways: first of all, as one element in a language system, whose 'meaning' is dependent on its relationships with the other words in the system. Secondly, its 'meaning' is linked up with a certain recognisable object in the external world.

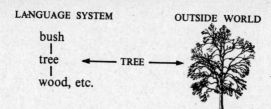

LANGUAGE SYSTEM   OUTSIDE WORLD

   bush
    |
   tree ←——— TREE ———→
    |
   wood, etc.

To the linguist, these two aspects are complementary—he examines first one, then the other, starting with the **internal** relationships between linguistic elements.

Lexical and Grammatical Meaning

In a sentence such as:

> Did you read about the boa constrictor which escaped from the zoo?

a linguist has to take into account at least two different types of meaning: **lexical** meaning and **grammatical** meaning. (This distinction was noted in Chapter 6.)

Lexical meaning involves individual lexical items which have 'content', as *read*, *boa constrictor*, *escape*, *zoo*. Note that lexical items do not correspond to orthographical words. *Boa constrictor*, for example, is two orthographical words, but is treated as a single lexical item.

Grammatical meaning refers mainly to the meaning of grammatical items such as *did*, *which*, *-ed*. It also includes the 'meaning' of sentence types, such as interrogative or imperative. In the sentence above, the query implied by the question mark is part of grammatical meaning. Grammatical meaning may also cover notions such as 'subject' and 'object'.

Because of its complexity, grammatical meaning is extremely difficult to study. As yet, no theory of semantics has been able to cope with it adequately.

But the study of lexical items is more manageable.

As with all linguistic elements, every lexical item has its own particular place in the pattern. By studying the relationships of individual items, a linguist can build up a picture of the overall structure of a language's vocabulary.

Collocation and Set

When a linguist studies the internal relationships of a lexical item, he must forget that the external world exists. He must forget that a word such as *apple* is an objectively identifiable object in the outside world, and must concentrate solely on its relationships with the other items within the language.

He can begin to build up a 'grid' of relationships by studying items which frequently occur with it (syntagmatic relationships, see Chapter 2) and items which can replace it (paradigmatic relationships).

When studying the structure of the vocabulary, **collocation** refers to the syntagmatic relationships of lexical items (derived from the Latin *colloco* 'to be in the same place with'). **Set** refers to paradigmatic relationships.

Collocation can be defined as the association of a lexical item with other lexical items.

Apple, for example, collocates with (is found with) words such as *eat, rosy, juicy*. *Red* collocates with *roses, blood*. *Sea* collocates with *rough, cruel, raging, blue*. *Mountain* collocates with words such as *climb, steep, peak*.

COLLOCATION

(syntagmatic)

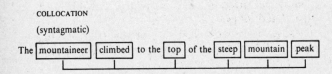

But beware. Cliches can mislead in a study of collocation. Phrases such as *dark horse, once in a blue moon, sky-blue pink* are comparable to single lexical items. The whole phrase cannot be satisfactorily dissected.

A **lexical set** is a group of lexical items from a similar class which seem to belong together. Each item in a set is defined by its place in relation to the other members of the set. *Adolescent*, for example, is the stage of growth between *child* and *adult*. *Cool* is the temperature between *cold* and *warm*. *Wood* comes between *copse* and *forest:*

SET

(paradigmatic)

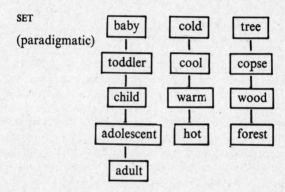

Such a study can give a very clear picture of the way in which a semantic field is divided up—though it is wrong to assume that lexical items cover an entire field like a smooth mosaic. In fact, they often overlap, leave gaps and have fuzzy edges.

In addition, this type of analysis pays little attention to the difference between so-called **denotation** and **connotation**—between what is sometimes thought of as the 'central' meaning of a word and its 'emotional overtones'.

Adolescent, for example, sometimes refers merely to a person of a certain age. But it often implies as well that the person referred to is awkward, immature, obstinate and moody.

Synonyms and Opposites

The **synonyms** and **opposites** of a word can give valuable insights into its relationships with the rest of the vocabulary.

Lexical items can be regarded as synonymous if they can be interchanged without altering the meaning of an utterance:

> e.g. He snapped the twig in half.
> He broke the twig in half.

By studying interchangeable items, a linguist can build up a picture of those with similar meanings.

But note that perfect synonymy is rare. That is, it is very unusual for two lexical items to have exactly the same meanings in all contexts. Occasionally, such synonymy is found between different registers (register = specialised usage; see Chapter 13). For example, *rubella* is the term found in medical literature for the disease that is more generally known as *German measles*.

Usually, a lexical item only partially overlaps another, and the two are synonymous only in certain contexts. For example:

> He snapped his fingers

does not mean the same as

> He broke his fingers.

And although

> He broke the record for the 100 yard sprint

is an acceptable sentence,

He snapped the record for the 100 yard sprint

would seem unusual to most English speakers.

The study of opposites is more complex, as there are several different types of opposites. For this reason, the word antonym has been avoided. Some writers use it for all types of opposite, others for one kind only.

The most obvious type is a pair of words in which the negative of one implies the other:

> he is not *married*: he is *single*
> he is not *single*: he is *married*.

A second type of opposite is one which is not absolute, but relative to some standard. *Small* and *large*, for example, mean nothing by themselves, but always imply some comparison:

> What a large mouse! (= what a large mouse in comparison to a normal size mouse)
> What a small elephant! (= what a small elephant in comparison to a normal size elephant)

A third type is when one word is the converse of the other. The choice of one opposite rather than another depends on the angle from which you view it:

> I *give* you the book: you *take* the book.

Classification (Inclusion)

A further way of examining vocabulary structure is to note the ways in which a language **classifies** items.

In English, for example, *dogs* and *cats* are classified as *domestic animals. Lions* and *tigers* are classified as *wild animals.* Both *domestic* and *wild* animals are classified together under the general heading of *animals.* And *animals* and *human beings* both come under the heading of *animate beings.*

The vocabulary of English is classified in this way in Roget's *Thesaurus*. Each entry has under it a list of **hyponyms** (i.e. things classified under it). This is one of the most interesting and linguistically useful reference books available. Its main drawback is that it does not distinguish between any stylistic or social variables which control the choice of synonyms.

Componential Analysis

The study of collocation, sets, synonyms, opposites and classification enables a useful grid of internal relationships between lexical items to be drawn up.

But there still remains a problem. How, in a semantic analysis, can one account for the fact that lexical items overlap? *Cow* and *woman* and *tigress*, for example, all contain some element of *femaleness*. *Bull* and *cow* both contain an element of *bovineness*. *Calf* and *puppy* and *baby* all contain an element of *non-adultness*.

Such reasoning has led to attempts to split items up into their component parts, or features. *Woman*, for example, is said to contain the semantic features of FEMALE, HUMAN, ADULT. *Cow* has the features of FEMALE, BOVINE, ADULT.

This type of analysis is comparable to distinctive feature analysis in phonology (see Chapter 5). But it is not new—a similar procedure is commonplace in dictionaries. For example, the *Concise Oxford Dictionary* defines a *mare* as 'female of equine animal'. But this technique has only recently begun to be exploited by linguists, and is known as **componential analysis.**

Hierarchical Structure of Semantic Features

Several attempts have been made recently to classify the features in certain fields into a **hierarchy,** in which more general features appear near the top and more specific ones lower down:

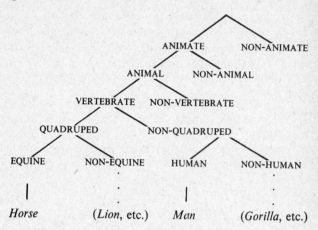

It is obvious, from the diagram above, that the number of semantic features varies from lexical item to lexical item. Fairly general items such as *human being*, *animal*, *foodstuff* have relatively few components. But more specific items such as *bus-conductor*, *giraffe*, *cheese* have a larger number.

And more specific features (features low down on the tree) imply more general features (features higher up on the tree). So the feature EQUINE implies also the features QUADRUPED, VERTEBRATE, ANIMAL and ANIMATE.

Are Binary Splits Always Possible?

In formulating a hierarchy of this kind, several problems arise. One problem is that of subdividing.

The diagram above showed a succession of **binary** splits (i.e. splits into two). One branch showed the presence of a feature, the other the absence.

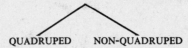

QUADRUPED   NON-QUADRUPED

This represents a fundamental characteristic of language—a tendency to organise items into pairs. We find, for example, *black* and *white*, *up* and *down*, *hot* and *cold*, *give* and *take*, *child* and *adult*, *lion* and *lioness*, *dead* and *alive*.

In a componental analysis, such pairs can be explained by the suggestion that each member of a pair differs from the other by only one feature. *Child*, for example, can be distinguished from *adult* by the presence or absence of the feature ADULT:

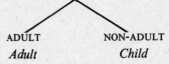

ADULT   NON-ADULT
Adult   *Child*

Lion can be distinguished from *lioness* by the presence or absence of the feature MALE:

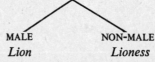

MALE   NON-MALE
Lion   *Lioness*

Dead can be distinguished from *alive* by the presence or absence of the feature LIVING:

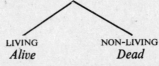

LIVING   NON-LIVING
Alive   *Dead*

A further interesting point in connection with some pairs is that one of the two may be more 'neutral' and general in its application, the other more specific.

In the sentence 'Lions live in Africa', the more general word *lion* is used to cover both the male and the female of the species. But *lioness* never refers to the male. The more general term is known as the **unmarked** member of a pair and the more specific one as the **marked** member.

Some linguists would like to extend the idea of pairing to cover the whole vocabulary, and would represent this in a componential analysis by successive binary splits.

But in some semantic fields pairs are difficult to identify—and may be non-existent. A notorious example is the field of colours.

With the exception of *black* and *white* (technically non-colours), colours appear to be organised in a continuous and partially overlapping spectrum (see page 101).

This causes problems for those who would like to organise all areas of vocabulary into a series of binary oppositions.

Cross-classifying Features

Another problem is that features cannot always be organised hierarchically. Well-known examples are the features MALE and ADULT. There is no reason to suppose that the feature ADULT is more general than the feature MALE—or that the feature MALE is more general than the feature ADULT. Neither implies the other, so they cannot be placed definitively on a hierarchy. They could be organised as follows:

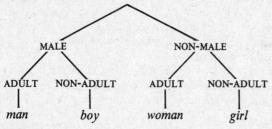

or as follows:

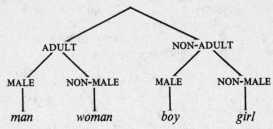

The same problem arises with regard to the features MALE and HUMAN, and ADULT and HUMAN. The feature MALE does not imply the feature HUMAN. There are male dogs, lions, porpoises, etc. Nor does the feature HUMAN imply MALE. Humans can also be female.

Features such as these which cannot be hierarchically classified in relation to one another are known as **cross-classifying** features.

Are Semantic Features Universal?

The recent upsurge of interest in componential analysis is partially due to the use of this technique by transformational grammarians.

It has been suggested that the lexicon attached to a transformational grammar should consist of items formed from a store of semantic features.

In the store, features such as MALE, ADULT, BOVINE, LIQUID, etc., are found. Each language selects relevant features, and puts them together to form its own lexical items. English would select BOVINE and NON-ADULT for *calf*, for example.

The implication is that such semantic features are universal—and the reason languages differ in vocabulary is because they put the features together in different combinations. The most extreme supporters of this theory suggest that semantic features are actually imprinted on the brain in some way.

Other linguists regard this idea as unlikely: reality seems far too complex. Languages, they say, do not focus on logical, physical semantic features, but select those which have importance for their particular culture.

Few speakers of any language, they argue, regard a cow as a combination of female, bovine and adult. An English speaker is more likely to note features connected with cud chewing and the provision of milk. In India, where cows are sacred, a totally different set of features would be relevant. In fact, an Englishman and an Indian possibly perceive cows quite differently. Such questions are still under discussion.

Compatibility and the Meaning of Sentences

The lexical items of a language, then, form a coherent pattern. They are not as rigidly organised as rules of grammar, but sufficiently patterned to enable each item to have a definable relationship with all the other items.

But how do human beings put these items together into sentences, interweaving them with each other and with rules of grammar?

It is obviously wrong to assume that we understand sentences by gradually learning all possible permutations of words, since we frequently come across totally new sentences which we have never heard before and understand them.

What a human has learned is not an inventory of all possible sentences, but a series of semantic rules which enable him to make meaningful sentences.

These rules seem likely to be, in part, rules of **compatibility.** *Pregnant* and *woman* are obviously compatible elements in a sentence, whereas *pregnant* and *bachelor* are incompatible. Similarly *colourless* and *green* are incompatible, but *green* and *grass* or *green* and *colourful* are compatible. Exactly how these compatibility rules work is uncertain—but the suggestion that compatible items have some common semantic feature is the most promising approach so far.

These rules of compatibility apply not only to compatibility between lexical items, but also to compatibility between lexical items and grammatical elements. A past tense is compatible with the word *yesterday:* 'I went to the theatre yesterday', but incompatible with the word *tomorrow:* 'I went to the theatre tomorrow'.

Further research into the integration of grammatical and lexical meaning is currently occupying the attention of many linguists. It has been suggested that every lexical item has inbuilt instructions regarding its use. These instructions would be of two types, grammatical and semantic.

The *grammatical* instructions might specify certain grammatical conditions which apply whenever an item is used. The verb *eat*, for example, must have a subject and must have an object:

subject ◄————| EAT |————► object

Note that these instructions apply to the deep structure only. The object of *eat* can sometimes be deleted in the surface structure (see Chapter 7).

The *semantic* instructions might indicate features which must be present in the associated items mentioned in the grammatical instructions. *Eat* would have a rule stating that the subject must be ANIMATE and the object EDIBLE:

subject ◄————| EAT |————► object

ANIMATE   EDIBLE

Internal versus External Meaning

So far, meaning has been treated as a system of internal relationships—lexical items have been defined by their relationships with other items.

This treatment of language as a self-contained system is essential as a first step—and is the aspect of meaning on which most work has been done.

But a full study of meaning requires a second step also. The meaning of an utterance must be examined in relation to the external world.

The link up of a word with the outside world is complex.

At least two important facts have emerged. Firstly, boundaries are never clear-cut. Every word appears to have a certain 'hard core' of meaning on which most speakers would agree. If an English speaker is asked to identify the colour of blood, he would probably say *red*. But if asked to name the colour of the setting sun, some would say *red*, others *orange*.

So the hard core of agreement fades away into a fuzzy edge, where words overlap.

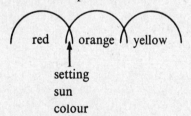

It is impossible to be more precise because a speaker is inconsistent in his use of words. He might name the setting sun *red* if he was contrasting it with the colour *blue*. But he might call it *orange* if he were trying to contrast it with the colour of blood.

The second important fact is that one-word utterances are rare—it is misleading to study the external world item by item. The whole surrounding **context of situation** must be examined as a structural whole.

A large number of utterances, particularly those associated with everyday activity or ritual, cannot usefully be dissociated from this overall context of situation.

The first person to study meaning in this way was the anthropologist Malinowski. He pointed out, for example, that when Trobriand Islanders go fishing everything they say is intimately linked up with the accompanying action and surroundings.

His idea was taken up by J. R. Firth, who started to draw up a rough schema of the things a linguist should note for a full understanding of the context of situation: the relevant features and actions of the participants in a conversation, for example, and the effect of an utterance.

Firth pointed out that the same contexts of situation tend to recur in society. In certain typical situations, it is possible to predict roughly what someone will say. This observation has important implications for sociolinguistics (see Chapter 13)—and it is sociolinguists and anthropologists who are most concerned with studying contexts of situation. But, so far, no adequate framework has been worked out for this.

QUESTIONS

1. Distinguish between **lexical** and **grammatical** meaning.
2. Distinguish between **collocation** and **set**.
3. Distinguish three types of **opposites** found in language.
4. What is **componential analysis?**
5. What is meant by the **hierarchical structure** of semantic features?
6. What is meant by **context of situation?**

PART THREE

LANGUAGE CHANGE

*There was no light nonsense about Miss Blimber . . .
She was dry and sandy with working in the graves of
deceased languages. None of your live languages for
Miss Blimber. They must be dead—stone dead—and
then Miss Blimber dug them up like a ghoul.*

Charles Dickens

CHAPTER 10

Comparative Historical Linguistics

The term 'comparative linguistics' is often used vaguely and inaccurately to cover a variety of linguistic activities.

Linguists compare languages for several reasons. A linguist may compare two (or more) languages in order to note their dissimilarities. This is normally called **contrastive** linguistics. It is useful for pinpointing the difficulties a beginner might encounter when learning a foreign language.

Or he may compare languages because he is interested in **typology**—the classification of languages into different types. He might, for example, classify all tone languages together, or all languages which use word order as a syntactic device.

Thirdly, a linguist may compare languages which are genetically related—that is, those that have developed from some common source. This is **comparative historical linguistics.** By comparing related forms, it is possible to draw conclusions about the history of a language long before the time of the first written texts.

Comparative historical linguistics may be said to have begun in 1786, the date when Sir William Jones made his famous speech pointing out that Greek, Latin, Sanskrit, Celtic and Germanic appeared to have sprung from a common source (see Chapter 3). It was developed throughout the nineteenth century, and little of importance has been added since then.

The old name for the subject was **comparative philology** (it is still called this on several university syllabuses). This name causes confusion. In the U.S.A., France and Germany, 'philology' normally refers to the study of literary texts, not to comparative historical linguistics.

Parent and Daughter Languages

The original language from which a group of related languages are descended is the **parent** language, or the **proto-**language (as in Proto-Indo-European). Occasionally, the German word **Ursprache** is found (several famous nineteenth century scholars were of German nationality).

The descendants of a parent language are **daughter** languages, and related languages are referred to as **cognates** (from the Latin *cognatus* 'relative').

Every language, everywhere, is continually changing. So daughter languages gradually split off and move away from the form of the parent language. Comparative historical linguistics attempts to chart those changes.

The break-up of a parent language tends to occur when it becomes spread over a wide geographical area. New administrative centres spring up far away from the original administrative centre. The language gradually splits into different dialects radiating from the new centres.

The pull of a language based on an administrative centre is like the ever widening and weakening ring of ripples formed by a pebble dropped in a pond. The further away from the centre you move, the less its influence is felt.

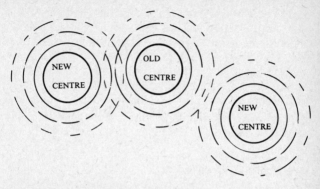

Assumptions Underlying Comparative Historical Linguistics

Two basic assumptions underlie comparative historical linguistics.

Firstly, **linguistic symbols are essentially arbitrary.** There is no connection between the sound of a word and the thing it symbolises, except in the case of occasional onomatopoeic words (see Chapter 1). This means that any consistent similarities between languages which cannot be explained by borrowing must be due to common origin.

The second assumption is the **regularity of sound 'laws'.** If one sound changes, then all similar sounds in a similar phonetic environment and geographical area change also (see Chapters 3, 11). So reliable and systematic correspondences can be drawn up between the various related languages.

Recognition of Related Languages

The first task is to establish which languages are related to one another. This is not as easy as it may seem, since borrowed words complicate the picture. Similar lexical items must be ignored—or treated with great caution—as these are often due to chance or borrowing. It is chance, for example, that the German word *haben* 'have' resembles Latin *habere* 'have'. And English borrowed the word *camp* from the Latin *campus* 'plain'.

The best evidence for related languages is **systematic correspondences in the phonology and morphology** of the languages concerned.

Phonological Correspondences

The first thing to look for are systematic sound correspondences between words with the same or a similar meaning.

GERMAN			ENGLISH
d /d/		corresponds to	th /θ/
dick	'fat'	←——→	*th*ick
Ding	'thing'	←——→	*th*ing
Ba*d*	'bath'	←——→	ba*th*

schw /ʃv/	.	corresponds to	sw /sw/
*schw*immen	'swim'	←——→	*sw*im
*schw*ingen	'swing'	←——→	*sw*ing
*Sch*wan	'swan'	←——→	*sw*an

zw /tsv/		corresponds to tw /tw/
zweimal	'twice'	◄──────► twice
zwölf	'twelve'	◄──────► twelve
zwanzig	'twenty'	◄──────► twenty

pf /pf/		corresponds to p /p/
Pfeffer	'pepper'	◄──────► pepper
Pfanne	'pan'	◄──────► pan
Pfennig	'penny'	◄──────► penny

Such correspondences are the first clue that the languages may be related. The evidence is cumulative. The more correspondences, the more likely the languages are to be related.

But correspondences must never be accepted uncritically. We might be dealing with a series of loanwords which diverged in development after being borrowed. For example, there is a superficial correspondence between

French	*mouton* 'sheep'	English	*mutton*
	bouton 'button'		*button*
	glouton 'glutton'		*glutton*

But these are all words borrowed from French at the time of the Norman invasion.

Morphological Correspondences

Although languages often borrow lexical items, morphological borrowing is rare. So morphological correspondences provide the surest proof for identifying related languages.

GERMAN   corresponds

i /ɪ/ ~	a /a/ ~	u /ʊ/
sing	sang	gesungen
trink	trank	getrunken
sink	sank	gesunken

to ENGLISH

i /ɪ/ ~	a /æ/ ~	u /ʌ/
sing	sang	sung
drink	drank	drunk
sink	sank	sunk

GERMAN   corresponds

ø ø ~	-er /ə/ ~	-ste /ste/
klein	kleiner	kleinste
schnell	schneller	schnellste
reich	reicher	reichste

to ENGLISH

ø ø ~	-er /ə/ ~	-est /est/
small	smaller	smallest
quick	quicker	quickest
rich	richer	richest

Such correspondences definitely prove that German and English are related.

It was on the basis of morphological correspondences

that Hittite was established as an Indo-European language earlier in this century—in spite of the fact that its vocabulary consists mainly of non-Indo-European words.

Reconstruction of the Proto-language

After proving that several languages are related, the next stage is the reconstruction of the proto-language from which they have developed.

This is done by the so-called **comparative method.** Related forms are compared, and the most probable original form is reconstructed.

Three principles act as guide lines in this reconstruction: the **majority verdict, phonetic probability** and **pattern congruity.**

An example of how these principles work can be seen in the reconstruction of the Indo-European word for *seven* from the Greek, Latin and Sanskrit forms:

Sanskrit	sapta
Greek	hepta
Latin	septem

Step **(i)** *Majority Verdict*

Phoneme	1	2	3	4	5	6
Sanskrit	s	a	p	t	a	
Greek	h	e	p	t	a	
Latin	s	e	p	t	e	m
Majority verdict	s	e	p	t	a	ø

Taking each phoneme in turn, and selecting the one on which most languages agree, the provisional reconstruction is /*septa/.[1]

Step (ii) *Phonetic Probability*

By reconstructing a provisional *septa*, we have implied that certain changes took place.

The next step is to check whether, in theory, such changes are phonetically likely. (Note that the formula s > h means 's changes into h'.)

Phoneme 1 /s/ > /h/   Yes
       2 /a/ > /e/   Yes
       5 /e/ > /a/   Yes
       6 /ø/ > /m/   No

It is impossible for an original zero /ø/ to have become /m/. Far more likely would be /m/ > /ø/, i.e. loss of final /m/.

So the reconstruction can, tentatively, be amended to /*septam/.

Step (iii) *Pattern Congruity*

The final step is to check whether the proposed changes fit into the pattern one would expect for the languages concerned.

Phoneme 1 Indo-European /*s/ > Greek /h/   Yes
       2 Indo-European /*e/ > Sanskrit /a/   Yes
       5 Indo-European /*a/ > Latin /e/   Yes[2]
       6 Indo-European /*m/ > Greek /ø/   No
         Indo-European /*m/ > Sanskrit /ø/   No

---

[1] Reconstructed forms are marked with an asterisk * to indicate that they are never actually found.

[2] I.E. /*a/ only becomes Latin /e/ in certain positions in the word.

Greek and Sanskrit do not normally lose /m/ at the end of words—so something must be wrong somewhere.

But Greek and Sanskrit /a/ sometimes develop from I.E./m̩/[1] a sound that is half-consonant, half-vowel, like the syllable at the end of English *bottom*. And I.E. /m̩/ becomes Latin /em/, which fits the facts here.

So the final reconstruction is | * septm̩ |

Unreliability of Reconstructed Forms

Reconstructed forms are unlikely to be an accurate reproduction of the speech of the parent language. They represent the most probable reconstruction in the light of current knowledge.

There are several reasons for their inaccuracy. First of all, there are always enormous gaps in the evidence available. In the reconstruction of Proto-Indo-European, linguists rely overmuch on Greek and Latin because of the extensive written records, dating from around 1300 B.C. Similar written records of Albanian or Armenian might dramatically change the picture.

Secondly, reconstructions rely on written texts from which it is often impossible to deduce the original pronunciation. The reconstructed phonemic pattern may be reasonably reliably deduced—but the actual phonetic values will be imprecise. It is fairly evident that Indo-European had five short vowels /a/ /e/ /i/ /o/ /u/—but exactly how these were pronounced will never be known.

Thirdly, no parent language is ever a single, homogeneous whole. Every language has dialectal variations within it—so reconstructions are likely to be hotchpotch forms made up from several dialects.

---

[1] /m̩/ is written as /m̥/ in older texts which do not use the I.P.A.

Fourthly, daughter languages sometimes undergo independent, parallel developments, which can falsify the picture of the parent language. If we possessed only English, Russian and Italian, we might wrongly assume that Indo-European had a stress accent. But stress developed independently in all three languages after the break-up of the parent language.

The Value of Reconstructions

If reconstructions are inaccurate, non-phonetic and a dialectal hotch-potch, what is the point of making them?

The answer is twofold. First of all, and most important, reconstructed forms are a convenient way of summing up the correspondences between the various related languages. In de Saussure's words, a reconstruction can 'crystallise and condense a number of conclusions'. By looking at a reconstructed form beside its daughter language equivalents, inherited features can instantly be distinguished from innovations.

Secondly, reconstructed words can sometimes shed light on earlier civilisations. Although the reconstruction of any individual word is suspect, the general pattern underlying large numbers of reconstructed forms can be informative, both with regard to language and general cultural background.

Certain definite facts emerge about Indo-European. The phonemic pattern is fairly clear. Notable points are the large number of vowels and large number of stop consonants.

In the grammar, the clear-cut separation of nouns and verbs is one of its most distinctive characteristics. The noun had eight cases. And in the verb system, **aspect** was more important than tense. An action was classified as being incomplete, complete or a momentary happening—and this distinction was more important than that of past, present and future. There was a **dual,** for pairs, as well as the expected singular and plural.

Clues about the cultural background are provided by **semantic** reconstructions.

Semantic Reconstructions

Semantic reconstructions require a slightly different technique from phonological ones—meanings tend to shift, and it is often impossible or useless to apply 'majority verdict' or 'semantic probability' tests.

The first essential is to get rid of all preconceived notions—it is not necessarily true, for example, that words move from concrete to abstract applications (as was commonly believed in the nineteenth century). Secondly, a unifying thread behind the various daughter language meanings must be detected for each root.

Sometimes a semantic reconstruction is obvious. The Greek God *Zeus* (who lived in the sky), Sanskrit *dyaus* 'sky', Latin *dies* 'day' and the Roman god *Jupiter* all come from the same root, which appears to mean *sky*. Presumably, the Indo-Europeans worshipped natural forces, and in particular a sky god.

Other reconstructions are less obvious—the English words *dough, paradise* and *fiction* are all phonologically connected. *Dough* is closely linked with a Gothic word 'to mould'. *Fiction* is a loanword from Latin, also derived from a verb meaning 'to mould'. *Paradise* is a loanword, via Greek, from Avestan (old Iranian) meaning 'a walled-garden'. How can the sense of *mould* and *walled garden* be reconciled? A closer look reveals that Avestan *pairidaeza* originally meant 'a surrounding wall'—derived from a word meaning 'to build'. So here an original I.E. *deigh 'to make' can be postulated, which became 'to mould' in western daughter languages and 'to build' in eastern ones.

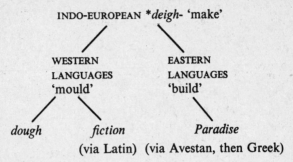

INDO-EUROPEAN *deigh*- 'make'

WESTERN   EASTERN
LANGUAGES   LANGUAGES
'mould'   'build'

dough   *fiction*   *Paradise*
        (via Latin) (via Avestan, then Greek)

Often, in order to make a satisfactory reconstruction, minor uses and obscure derivatives must be examined, as well as the main descendants of an I.E. root. A Greek word meaning 'flower' corresponds to a Sanskrit word meaning 'fodder'. The problem of the original meaning is solved by looking at Greek medical literature. There, a verb derived from the same root refers to the growth of hair—also to skin eruptions. The Greek word for 'straw' is also connected. So, probably, the original I.E. word referred to 'shoot, sprout, upward growth'— and eventually became specialised as 'flower' in Greek and 'fodder' in Sanskrit.

In addition, a semantic reconstruction must fit into the general semantic pattern. It would be useless to reconstruct a word meaning 'iron' for Proto-Indo-European because all other reconstructions point to a pre-Iron Age civilisation.

It is this general pattern which provides information about the culture of the speakers of a proto-language.

Reconstruction of a Culture

The broad outlines of a culture can be built up from the general pattern which is formed from the accumulated individual reconstructions.

A fairly convincing picture of our Indo-European ancestors emerges.

They lived in a patriarchal society. Apart from the immediate family, all reconstructable non-immediate relatives belonged to the man, not to the woman: husband's mother, husband's father, husband's sister, husband's brother, husband's brother's wife and so on. This is consistent with a society in which a wife leaves her own home on marriage and acquires her husband's relatives.

A decimal system was in use. Numbers one to ten can be fairly accurately reconstructed, and numbers ten to one hundred are derived from them.

Natural forces were personified and worshipped— particularly the sky. Bronze was a well-known metal, and the wheel had been invented.

The geographical location of this culture is less certain. The evidence is based mainly on words relating to plants and animals.

Trying to locate the Indo-Europeans was a fashionable activity during the nineteenth and early twentieth centuries. It was closely connected with national pride, since various writers (particularly German ones) attempted to prove that their own homeland was the 'Indo-European cradle'. This type of study was known as the **Wörter-und-Sachen** technique or **linguistic palaeontology.**

The flora and fauna vocabulary of Indo-European indicates a homeland somewhere in central, eastern or northern Europe. Further pin-pointing is a matter of dispute. The arguments centre round the words for 'beech' *bhagos* and 'salmon' *laks*.

Beech trees do not grow east of the Baltic Sea, and salmon are found only in rivers running into the Baltic and German Sea. So the evidence apparently points to a community based on the Baltic and North German plains in the late Stone and Bronze Ages.

But this 'proof' is highly unreliable. It does not allow for the possibility of semantic change. Beech trees are not found in Greece, but the I.E. word *bhagos* is found applied to an oak tree. And the I.E. word *laks* means 'fish' in Toccharian (East Turkestan). So we have no absolute proof that our reconstructions of 'beech' and 'salmon' are correct. Perhaps Greek and Toccharian preserve more ancient meanings.

The absence of words referring to certain eastern or southern animals is sometimes taken as further proof of a North German location. But this ignores the possibility of taboo. In primitive societies, words frequently disappear for superstitious reasons—particularly the names of animals. The I.E. word for 'bear' is missing in Germanic and Balto-Slavonic. Instead, periphrases meaning 'the brown one' or 'honey eater' are found. This development may be due to taboo.

All in all, broad outlines rather than exact details are all that can be expected from attempts to reconstruct a culture.

QUESTIONS

1. How are **related languages** identified?
2. What principles should be followed when making a **phonological reconstruction?**
3. Why are reconstructed forms unreliable?
4. What is the point of making reconstructions?
5. How do **semantic reconstructions** differ from phonological ones?
6. What is **linguistic palaeontology?**

CHAPTER 11

Sound Change

All languages are continually changing—their sounds, their grammar and their meaning.

This gradual alteration is unnoticed by most speakers of a language. The sounds especially give a superficial impression of being static. Yet one glance at Chaucer or Shakespeare shows how much English sounds have changed in a relatively short time.

A closer look at English reveals several sounds in the process of changing. The y-sound (phonetically [j]) which occurs before /u/ in words such as *tune*, *muse*, *duty* is dropping out. It has already disappeared in words such as *rule*, *lute*. Soon, it may have dropped out entirely, as in American English.

But the astonishing thing about language is not the fact that it changes, but that it changes so little, and in such an orderly fashion.

No change ever upsets the basic design characteristics of human language. No language has ever disintegrated through a series of changes. There is some unconscious mechanism which enables a language to retain its equilibrium.

Sound changes are not random, disruptive events, but highly ordered and well integrated alterations.

The mechanisms of sound change are still very imperfectly understood. A linguist approaches the problem by dividing the study of sound changes into two complementary tasks. First of all, he describes a change. Secondly, he attempts to interpret it by examining its possible causes.

Description of Sound Changes: Extent of a Change

Sound changes are regular. Normally, when one sound changes, all similar sounds in the same phonetic environment and the same geographical area change at the same time.

But the extent of such changes varies considerably—in time, in geographical area and in the number of conditioning factors.

A change may continue in operation for well over a century—or it may operate for a short time only. It may be limited to one particular village, or it may be spread over thousands of miles.

It may affect a sound every time it occurs in a language—or it may affect it only under a limited set of conditions.

It is difficult to assign changes to types, since there are always borderline cases which do not fit any scheme. But, as a rough guide, changes can be placed in one of three categories:

   (i) **unconditioned** (or generic) changes
   (ii) **conditioned** (or combinatory) changes
   (iii) **sporadic** changes.

Conditioned and Unconditioned Changes

An **unconditioned** change is a change which affects every occurrence of a certain sound, no matter whereabouts in the word it occurs.

Old English /aː/ (long a) changes everywhere to Middle English /oː/ (and later to /əʊ/):

$$\text{O.E. } /\text{aː}/ > \text{M.E. } /\text{oː}/.$$

The word *hām*, for example, became *hoom* (and later *home*). Evidence of the old word for 'home' is found in place names such as Clapham, Frensham. Similarly, the word *bān* became *boon*, and later bone.

Unconditioned changes are rare. **Conditioned** changes are much commoner. These are changes which occur only under a fixed set of conditions.

These conditions vary. They may be connected with the place of a sound within the word—a change may only occur in initial syllables. For example, in Middle English, the first syllable of any three-syllable word was shortened, so *hāligdaeg* eventually became *holiday*.

Or the change may depend on the sounds either side of it—Middle English /e/ became /a/ before /r/:

> sterre   starre   (star)
> derk   dark.

The list of such minor changes is endless. Superficially, they may appear pointless—but, on closer examination, similar changes recur in different languages. [r] frequently causes the vowels near it to move towards [a] (as in *star*, *dark*, above). A vowel before [ŋ] moves towards [i], as in the word *England*.

Close attention to what people are actually saying (ignoring the conventional spelling of a word) is a very useful guide to phonetic tendencies.

Sporadic Change: Assimilation and Dissimilation

It is difficult to draw the line between conditioned change and **sporadic** change, since the two merge into one another.

The word 'sporadic' is usually applied when a particular sequence of phonemes leads to a change that does not occur elsewhere. It is in reality a conditioned change in which very rigid conditions apply.

The most important type of sporadic change is **assimilation** (from the Latin 'to become like'). It occurs when one sound is influenced by a neighbouring sound to such an extent that it moves phonetically in the direction of this neighbour.

Assimilation may be **complete** or **partial.**

In the word *immense*, from *in-mensus* 'un-measurable', [n] has become completely assimilated to [m].

But in *imbibe*, from *in-bibo* 'drink in', [n] has been only partially assimilated to the [b]. It has altered until it is pronounced in the same part of the mouth (assimilation of place of articulation), but has not been completely assimilated.

The assimilated sound can occur before or after the sound which influences it. The most common type is **regressive** assimilation, when a sound is assimilated to the following sound. Regressive assimilation is so called because the influential sound is visualised as travelling back towards the beginning of the word:

in ⟨ m ⟩ ensus   i ⟨ mm ⟩ ensus.

Progressive assimilation, when the influential sound seems to be travelling forwards, is far less common. It is found in the English past tense, when the final /d/ is partially assimilated to a previous voiceless sound:

/hel ⟨ p ⟩ d/   /hel ⟨ pt ⟩ /.

The opposite of assimilation is **dissimilation,** which occurs when two similar sounds become dissimilar. The word *pilgrim* is from the Latin *peregrinus*, but the first [r] has become [l]. Dissimilation of two [r] sounds is very common, as it is physically difficult to say [r] several times in quick succession, and the speech organs tend to avoid such tongue twisters.

Sporadic Change Involving Consonants

There are various other types of sporadic change. The most important types involving consonants are **transposition, haplology, excrescence, loss, wrong word division** and **spelling pronunciation**:

1. **Transposition** (or metathesis)

   Two sounds change place:

   wæps > *wasp* with transposition of /p/ and /s/. The form *wopsie* is a dialectal variant which did not undergo this change.

2. **Haplology** (from the Greek word meaning 'single')

   When two similar syllables occur together, one is sometimes lost:

   Engla-lond > *England*
   morphophonemic > *morphonemic*.

3. **Excrescence** (from the Latin 'to grow out of')

   The addition of an extra sound:

   bremel > *brembel* (later *bramble*) with excrescent /b/.

4. **Loss**

   The loss of a consonant from a cluster of consonants in order to make pronunciation easier. Many people do not pronounce the /p/ in *attempt*:

   /ətempt/ > /ətemt/.

5. **Wrong word division**

   Words occasionally get wrongly divided, especially in non-literate societies:

   a nadder > *an adder*
   an ewt > *a newt*.

6. **Spelling pronunciation**

   In literate societies, people occasionally pronounce words as they are spelt:

   faute > *fault*.

The word *faute* was borrowed from the French. When intellectuals discovered its connection with Latin *fallo* 'to make a mistake', *l* was incorporated in the spelling. This gradually crept into the pronunciation.

Sporadic Change Involving Vowels

The three most important types of sporadic change involving vowels are **syncope, apocope,** and **anaptyxis.**

1. **Syncope** (from the Greek 'to cut from the middle, shorten')

   The loss of a vowel from the middle of a word:

   capitain > *captain.*

   Capitain was borrowed from French, with later syncope of the /i/.

2. **Apocope** (from the Greek 'to cut off')

   The loss of a vowel from the end of a word:

   helpe > *help.*

3. **Anaptyxis** (from the Greek 'unfolding')

   The insertion of an extra vowel:

   knīf > *canif* 'knife'.

   The French borrowed the German *knīf*, but inserted an extra vowel.

Description of Sound Changes: Splits and Mergers

Another way in which a change can be described is in terms of the re-arrangement of phonemes. Two basic types of re-arrangement are **splits** and **mergers.**

A **merger** is the joining together of two separate phonemes into one new one.

English in Shakespeare's time had two different long e-vowels, /eː/ (similar to the vowel in French *thé*) and /ɛː/ (similar to the vowel in *pen*). These two merged into a single phoneme:

/meːt/   mɛːt/   **MERGER**
meet   meat

A **split** is the division of a phoneme into two.

English /ŋ/ is, today, a separate phoneme—but it used to be an allophone of /n/, occurring before /k/ and /g/. When people stopped pronouncing /g/ at the end of words, minimal pairs such as *ran* and *rang* (/ræn/ and /ræŋ/) resulted. So /ŋ/ became a new phoneme:

/n/

SPLIT

/n/   /ŋ/

The split and merger picture is not always straight-forward—quite often a sound change involves both splitting *and* merging. Part of one phoneme splits off and merges with another. The vowel in *swan* was once [æ]. But after [w], [æ] became [ɒ]:

/swæn/ > /swɒn/.

The resulting /ɒ/ then merged with the already existing phoneme /ɒ/:

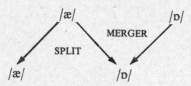

/æ/   /ɒ/

MERGER

SPLIT

/æ/   /ɒ/

The importance of this type of description is that it looks at a sound change in relation to the other phonemes in a language. No sound change is an isolated incident. In an interconnected system, a change in one item automatically affects all the other items by a chain reaction.

The Causes of Sound Change

There is no one reason why sounds change. When the factors surrounding a change are analysed, there are usually several contributory reasons.

Broadly, reasons for change can be assigned to one of two types of cause—**internal** and **external.**

With **internal** change, the key to the change lies within the system. **External** change is due to some kind of outside influence.

Linguists differ as to which of these types of cause is the more important. In fact, they complement one another. Possibly an external factor causes imbalance within the language system. This imbalance triggers off a series of re-adjustments which may take centuries to complete, since each one will trigger off further changes in a chain reaction. Examples of such happenings will be given in the sections below.

Internal Change: Language as a Self-regulating System

The phonemes of a language form an intricate pattern in which the different elements balance one another.

This type of patterning is the way in which the brain is able to handle large amounts of linguistic information without strain. If the patterning broke down, the brain would be overloaded with a junk heap of disorganised information and communication would be impossible.

Every language appears to have an unconscious desire to perfect its patterns—a never-ending struggle to stop up gaps and re-arrange everything into an ideal state. Language, like a thermostat, is **self-regulating,** constantly re-adjusting itself in an attempt to maintain an equilibrium.

But a perfect state can never be achieved—for a variety of reasons.

Irregular Layout of the Speech Organs

The first and most obvious reason why language never reaches a state of equilibrium is the layout of the human speech organs.

The speech organs are irregular in shape, and sounds are produced by a wide variety of different means: some with the teeth, others with the lips, some through the nose—and so on.

Sounds which are pronounced close together in the mouth can get confused in rapid speech, like [θ] and [f]. (Note Cockney *fink* for *think*.)

Other sounds, such as [r] and [l], are acoustically similar—these can also get misheard in fast speech.

Some sounds are stabler than others. [m] and [n] are stabler than [s] and [h]. Unstable sounds tend to be pressurised by the sounds either side of them in the flow of speech—and so are more subject to change.

So proximity, acoustic similarity and natural instability of sounds can all cause confusion and change—and any change will automatically set off a series of new changes as the system tries to re-adjust itself and regain its equilibrium.

Disharmony Between Different Levels

A sound system might, theoretically, achieve an optimal state in which phonemes were arranged in the best way possible in accordance with the shape of the vocal tract.

But sounds are only one level of language. They must be integrated with grammar and semantics. The requirements of grammar and semantics can sometimes upset the phonology.

In theory, language on all levels is working towards a state of perfect equilibrium in which all communication needs are satisfied by as simple a system as possible, with all levels co-operating in a common aim.

In practice, this state of maximum economy can never be achieved because the different levels do not work in harmony. A morphological change can affect the phonology—or a phonological change can have a disturbing effect on the morphology.

Redundancy

Another factor which makes a maximally simple system a practical impossibility is the need for **redundancy.**

In theory, long and complex words such as *transubstantiation* or German *Fahrradreparaturwerkzeuge* 'cycle repair outfit' are unnecessary. A language should, ideally, start with two phoneme words, such as *pa*, *ba*, *ta*, *po*, *bo*, *to*, etc. When all these are used up, it should proceed to three phoneme words and so on.

In practice, such a system would be unworkable.

When people speak, there are innumerable distractions and interruptions. They may hiccup in the middle, an aeroplane might pass overhead, a dog might bark. If every sound contained vital information, an important part would be lost out of almost every utterance. But if a word contains more clues to its identity than is strictly necessary, the non-hearing of an occasional sound does not matter.

So this superfluity of linguistic clues, or **redundancy,** is an important factor in language. A language without redundancy would be an inefficient tool of communication, since every message would have to be repeated two or three times to avoid misunderstandings.

Interpretation of a Change

Since language may be viewed as a self-regulating system, every change can be regarded either as a **disruption** of an existing equilibrium or as an attempt to **restore** the equilibrium.

The split of phoneme /n/ into /n/ and /ŋ/, for example, could be regarded as an attempt to restore harmony to the phonemic pattern by aligning /m n ŋ/ with /p t k/ and /b d g/. This underlying need for patterning could have unconsciously triggered off the *immediate* cause of the change—the loss of the conditioning phoneme (see page 125).

LABIAL	DENTAL	VELAR[1]
p	t	k
b	d	g
m	n	ŋ

On the other hand, the gradual loss of /t/ in British cockney might be interpreted as a disruption of a formerly stable pattern, whose cause must be looked for elsewhere (on another language level, or externally).

Yet the picture is never this simple. Numerous changes on all levels take place concurrently, and it is never easy to itemise out all the various factors involved. Perhaps an existing state of disequilibrium could be

[1] For explanations of the phonetic terms, see the Appendix. *Labial*, *dental* and *velar* all refer to places of articulation within the mouth.

solved in various ways—but language chooses one path rather than another for external reasons.

French /y/ as in *tu* 'you' (sg.) is a case in point. This was once pronounced [u] as in *vous*. A lack of balance in the vowel system made a change likely—but the form it took [u] > [y] was possibly stimulated by the fact that the sound [y] occurred in the surrounding Celtic languages.

Chain Reactions

Since all the items in language are interlinked, a change in any one is likely to trigger off a whole series of other changes.

A changing sound is likely to leave a hole in the sound pattern—so another sound moves in to fill the empty space. It in turn leaves a gap to be filled, and so on.

This may be what happened to the long vowels in Middle English. In Chaucer's time, the word *lyf* 'life' was pronounced [liːf] (like today's *leaf*). This vowel changed to [eɪ], leaving a gap where [iː] once was. This was filled by [eː] changing to [iː]. Then [ɛː] filled the empty space left by [eː], and [aː] filled the space left by [ɛː].[1]

This shift started off a series of changes which lasted for several centuries.

[1] With regard to the position of the tongue, there is only a small difference between [iː] and [eː], [eː] and [ɛː], [ɛː] and [aː]. For more information on the production of vowels, see the Appendix.

Yet the situation is not necessarily as straightforward as the example given here—which is itself disputed.

Quite often, several sounds move simultaneously—so it is impossible to say whether one sound is pulling another towards an empty space, or whether it is pushing another out of its rightful place. In the diagram below, is [eː] being **pulled** by [iː] or **pushed** by [ɛː]?

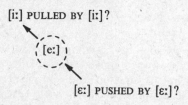

[iː] PULLED BY [iː]?

[eː]

[ɛː] PUSHED BY [ɛː]?

Controversy surrounds the actual mechanism by which such sounds affect one another. The only certain fact is that changes do seem to occur in linked sequences, and in so doing preserve the patterning so basic to human language.

Inhibition of Sound Changes

Sound changes are not totally like snow ploughs. The old belief that sound 'laws' work with 'blind necessity' sweeping all before them can be modified.

Sound changes are often interrupted or altered by **analogy,** defined as 'reasoning from parallel cases'. For example, we would expect *d* in the middle of the word *father* (as in Gothic *fadar*). But *father* was influenced by the word *brother*, and the expected *d* appears as *th* (/ð/). This type of change will be discussed in more detail in Chapter 12.

Note also that many apparent exceptions to sound changes disappear when the history of a word is examined more thoroughly.

On first sight, the words *bait* and *swain* (Old English *bāt* and *swān*) appear to be exceptions to the rule that O.E. /aː/ became /əʊ/, as /haːm/ > /həʊm/ (*hām* > *home*). But on closer examination *bait* and *swain* are not continuations of the Old English forms. They are borrowings from Scandinavian which took place after the Norse invasion of English.

Are Changes Sudden or Gradual?

Another controversial issue is the speed of sound change. Does a phoneme shift gradually from one sound to another? Or does it happen suddenly?

Some scholars are convinced that changes only occur between generations. Since language learning capacity declines rapidly at adolescence, they assume that all important changes are due to restructuring which takes place relatively early in a person's life. This may well be true of some changes—but by no means all.

Everybody varies his grammar and pronunciation slightly to suit the occasion. In rapid speech, a speaker might omit [h] at the beginning of *have* and [t] at the end of *but*—something he would perhaps not do in an interview or a radio talk.

New alternatives can creep in unnoticed throughout a person's life, since the majority of people unconsciously imitate those around them—a phenomenon frequently seen when Englishmen return from the U.S.A. with an American accent, and American constructions such as 'Do you use sugar?' and 'He's gotten married'.

When such alternatives exist in a speaker's repertoire, one sometimes ousts another if it is used often enough. It is then passed on to future generations.

Many changes can be regarded as spreading slowly, through social contact. A form used habitually by one group of people becomes a second, alternative form for others. Then this new alternative gradually ousts the older form.

A new alternative may differ from the old one by a very small amount—but it may set a tendency for change in a certain direction, a tendency carried further by the next generation.

So changes possibily occur in a number of minute, perhaps unnoticed but definite steps.

External Causes of Linguistic Change

No language exists in a vacuum—it is continually affected by external influences, other dialects and other languages with which it is in contact.

'Foreign' elements are continually interfering and causing disruptions.

From the point of view of the linguistic mechanisms involved, there is no difference between influence from a neighbouring dialect and that from a neighbouring language. The reasons for interference are usually social ones—so this type of study merges into sociolinguistics (see Chapter 13).

Sometimes, the gradual infiltration of a foreign element is unnoticed and unconscious—as in the gradual penetration of Arabic words and sounds into Turkish.

At other times, change can be a consciously planned phenomenon. Research has shown that in an area in New York regarded as being socially inferior its inhabitants have made a conscious and successful effort to imitate features in a socially respected dialect. The younger generation is growing up with these features firmly implanted in its speech.

External changes appear to penetrate gradually by appearing first as alternatives (often colloquial speech alternatives) and then gradually spreading. When the foreign elements are considered socially desirable, their acceptance and absorption is more rapid.

Overall Direction of Sound Change

Are sound changes causing languages to move in any definite direction? Since man is the product of evolution, one might expect to see some general evolutionary trend in language change.

But, so far, nothing has emerged.

Nineteenth century scholars tried to prove that certain morphological types were more advanced than others, but this appears to be unfounded (see Chapter 6).

A few twentieth century linguists have propounded a cyclical view of language change. They suggest that fusional languages lead to analytical ones and that agglutinating languages lead back to fusional ones (see Chapter 6). Certainly each of the various Indo-European languages seems to be working independently from a fusional to an analytical state—a fact which might support this view. But too little evidence exists to make firm judgments.

QUESTIONS

1. Distinguish between **unconditioned, conditioned** and **sporadic** change, and give examples of each.
2. Explain, giving examples, the difference between **splits** and **mergers.**
3. Distinguish between **internal** and **external** causes of linguistic change.
4. Why can language never achieve a state of perfect equilibrium?
5. What factors can inhibit sound change?
6. Discuss the speed of sound changes. Do they occur suddenly or gradually?

CHAPTER 12

Change in Grammar and Vocabulary

Grammatical change is often regarded as totally different in nature from sound change. Yet frequently it is motivated by the same driving force: the need to maintain and simplify the patterns of language in order to ease the load on the memory.

Analogy

The basic mechanism behind grammatical change is **analogy,** which, as already mentioned, can be defined as 'reasoning from parallel cases'.

The use of analogy—the ability to generalise a linguistic rule by applying it to similar cases—is a fundamental feature of human language. It is most obvious in the case of child language, when children form plurals such as *mans*, *mouses*, *foots* after hearing plurals such as *cats*, *dogs*, *horses*.

Through analogy, items which have a similar function tend to become similar in form. In English, the forms representing the plural morpheme have gradually become standardised. This reduces the total number of forms to remember and so eases the memory load.

At one time, English plurals mostly ended in either *-n* or *-s*. But *-n* has gradually been ousted in favour of *-s*. In Shakespeare, *eyen*, *housen* and *schoon* were still normal forms—but these have been replaced by *eyes*, *houses* and *shoes*. Today we retain only three forms in -*n*: *oxen*, *children* and *brethren* (besides the newer *brothers*).

Analogy appears to start with frequently recurring items, which then influence less frequent items. But why some common words start analogical trends, while others do not, is still a puzzle.

In the nineteenth century, it was suggested that all analogy could be explained by one simple ratio formula:

> pie : pies : : eye : x
> therefore x = eyes

(i.e. eye/eyes must be parallel to pie/pies).

In the twentieth century, linguists realise that the process is much more complex and is due to the interlocking of the numerous associations surrounding a word.

Associative Field

No word exists in isolation. Every word is enmeshed in a network of associations, its **associative field.**

De Saussure pointed out that every word is the centre of a constellation, at the point where an indefinite number of associated words converge. He illustrated this with a useful diagram:

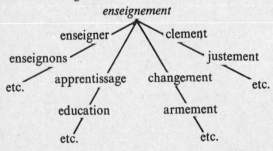

Each strand of associations is connected with a

different facet of the original word. Some sound the same, others are formed with the same morpheme, others are linked semantically. Each strand can potentially start off an analogical chain—resulting in several different types of analogy.

Types of Analogy

Various types of analogy can occur:

1. **Pure grammatical**

   e.g. English *eyen* > *eyes* after other plurals in *-s*.

2. **Semantic**

   e.g. *mâle*, *femelle* > *male*, *female*.

   English borrowed the French words *mâle* and *femelle*—but, owing to their semantic link, *femelle* became *female* under the influence of *male*.

3. **Back formation**

   e.g. *beg* from *beggar*, after pairs such as *sing*, *singer*.

   In back formation, a word is wrongly assumed to be derived from a base which never existed—but which is then created. So *beggar* was presumed to come from an originally non-existent verb *beg*.

4. **Wrong morpheme division**

   e.g. *cheeseburger*, *beefburger* after *hamburger*.

   Hamburgers originated in the town of Hamburg, hence their name, *hamburger*. This has been wrongly analysed into *ham-burger*, and has led to the detachment of the suffix *-burger* and the creation of new forms such as *beefburger*.

5. **Hypercorrection** (overcorrection)

   e.g. *Hamerica*, *Hoxford* (for America, Oxford).

Speakers who normally 'drop their aitches' often overcorrect this tendency when they wish to impress people, and produce hypercorrect forms such as *Hamerica, Hoxford.*

6. Extension of alternant forms

e.g. *draw a picture,* pronounced [drɔːr ə pɪktʃə] with intrusive [r].

Words which are spelled with *-r* keep this *-r* before a vowel, but lose it before a consonant:

hear a sound [hɪər ə saʊnd]
but *hear noises* [hɪə nɔɪzɪz].

Alternate forms such as [hɪər] and [hɪə] then influenced other words which never had an *-r*, as *draw* which now has two forms [drɔːr] and [drɔː]:

draw a picture [drɔːr ə pɪktʃə]
draw pictures [drɔː pɪktʃəz].

Vocabulary Change (Lexical Change)

There is no rigid dividing line between grammatical change and vocabulary change. Quite often the two intersect, as with the development of *brothers* and *brethren.* A new plural *brothers* was formed by analogy after words such as *mothers, fathers, sisters.* The old word *brethren* was retained, but became restricted to a specialised religious sense.

The vocabulary of a language is more strictly known as the **lexis** of a language, and it is **lexical items** which are examined. This eliminates the problem of talking about 'words'. Phrases such as *turn on, go up* (which are two words) can be regarded as single lexical items (see Chapter 9).

It is sometimes helpful to subdivide lexical changes into three facets:

(i) **loss of lexical items**
(ii) **change of meaning**
(iii) **creation of new lexical items**

(though these cannot be regarded as watertight compartments).

Loss of Lexical Items: Internal Causes

Word loss can, like other aspects of language change, be divided into loss due to internal factors and loss due to external factors. **Homonymic clash, phonetic attrition** and the **need to shorten common words** are common internal causes.

Homonyms are words which have the same phonemic structure but different meanings, as with *pole* 'a long shaft of wood', *Pole* 'a native of Poland', *pole* as in North Pole, South Pole.

The existence of homonyms need not lead to word loss (as the above example shows). It only does so if the homonyms crop up in the same context and cause confusion, as in the homonymic clash between English *leten* and *letten*.

In English, two similar items *leten* 'to permit' and *letten* 'to hinder' became homonymous, both developing into *let*. As there were numerous contexts when the two could become confused, the second *let* (to hinder) dropped out of existence, except for two specialised uses. A *let* ball in tennis is one which is temporarily impeded by the top of the net. And the phrase 'without *let* or hindrance' is still found in legal terminology.

Phonetic attrition is less usual. Sometimes a word becomes so altered by sound change that it almost disappears. A well-known example is the Latin word *apem* 'bee' which became /e/ in French. /e/ was too short to be stable and was replaced by different, longer words such as *abeille* or *mouche à miel* in the various dialects.

The **need to shorten common words** is a type of attrition, a linguistic phenomenon known as **Zipf's law.** Zipf showed that common words tend to be shorter than uncommon ones. So words in frequent use tend to be shortened. *Refrigerator* becomes *fridge*, *television* becomes *tele* or *T.V.*, *aeroplane* becomes *plane*. Occasionally, a high-frequency word cannot easily be shortened. In this situation, the original word sometimes drops out and a shorter one is substituted. So *baby carriage* was replaced by *pram* (from *perambulator*). *Automobile* is dropping out in favour of *car*.

Loss of Lexical Items: External Causes

External causes of lexical loss are, broadly speaking, either **historical** or **social.**

Words such as *doublet*, *pikestaff*, *visor* have dropped out for **historical** reasons. These objects are no longer part of everyday life—so the words have gradually faded out of everyday use.

Social reasons are more diverse. Sometimes alternative lexical items are in use, depending on region or social class, as with pairs such as *table napkin* and *serviette*, *radio* and *wireless*. If one of the pair becomes more socially acceptable, the other is likely to drop out of use.

An interesting type of social cause is lexical loss through **taboo.** Sometimes, people intentionally avoid certain words due to superstitious fears or embarrassment. Today, many people speak of 'passing away' rather than *dying*, and of a 'malignant growth' rather than *cancer*.

American attempts to avoid the word *lavatory* (which itself originally meant a place to wash) has led to a list of substitutes such as *comfort station, powder room, little girls' room*.

Religious taboos are common, particularly in connection with forces of evil. People speak of 'the other place' rather than *hell*. And in French literature the *devil* is sometimes referred to as *l'Autre* 'the other one'.

Animal taboos occur all over the world. In certain rural districts of England, the word *rabbits* is avoided—and it is possibly due to taboo that the old word *coney* 'rabbit' was lost. The lack of the expected Indo-European word for *bear* in the Balto-Slavonic and Germanic language families may also be the result of a taboo (see Chapter 10).

Change of Meaning

The meaning of a lexical item can change in a variety of ways. Its meaning can be **restricted, extended** or **transferred.**

Restriction of meaning is found with the English word *meat* which once meant *food* in general.

Similarly, the word *deer* originally referred to any animal, as does its German cognate *Tier*.

Extension of meaning is less common than restriction. It is found in the word *arrive*, which is derived from the Latin *adripare* 'to come to the bank', i.e. 'to arrive by ship'. Now it means to arrive by any means of transport whatever. A similar development has taken place with the verb to *land*, which has now been extended to include landing on water:

The gull *landed* on the sea with a gentle splash.

Transfer of meaning is seen in the word *fee* which originally meant 'cattle', since cattle were once commonly used as payment. (Note the German cognate *Vieh* 'cattle'.) The word *pen* originally meant 'quill' or 'feather', since pens were once made of goose quills.

The **causes** of change of meaning are numerous.

No change can be studied in isolation. Each alteration is likely to cause, or be caused by, changes in related lexical items.

For example, in America the word *agony* now merely means 'inconvenience', as in 'Avoid the agony of being caught in a traffic jam'. This type of 'devaluation' of a word is common. It is brought about by frequent usage and journalistic attempts to liven up newspapers with vivid metaphors.

But, ultimately, such a shift in meaning will cause changes in the whole of a lexical set. A new word must eventually replace agony (*tragedy? heartbreak?*), and the word *inconvenience* will be further demoted as *agony* replaces it.

STAGE 1	Agony $\to$	Inconvenience	$\to$
STAGE 2	Tragedy	Agony	Inconvenience

So, since a change of meaning (like a sound change) is often one of a series of linked changes, the internal relationships of all words connected with the change must be carefully examined as a first priority. Then, afterwards, external factors must be studied in order to find a precipitating factor which might have triggered the series of changes.

New Lexical Items

The creation of new lexical items is conditioned partly by necessity, partly by fashion.

Necessity arises when a word is lost for linguistic reasons, such as attrition or homonymic clash. Obviously a new one must take its place. Similarly, if the meaning of a word is 'devalued', another one must be put in the gap left by the devalued one. And new inventions such as *radar*, *laser* and *penicillin* require new words.

But at other times new words arise purely through fashion. New alternatives spring up alongside older words. At first, these alternatives may be regarded as slang expressions. Few people nowadays refer to *marijuana*. Names such as *pot*, *hash*, *grass* are becoming increasingly common. (This may also be an example of Zipf's law—the tendency to shorten common words.)

The continual infiltration of new lexical items is a normal and healthy happening. It is related to the essential productivity of language—the ability to say new things and deal with new situations. Newspaper articles which deplore 'creeping Americanisms' as undermining 'the purity' of British English are sadly ignorant of the basic characteristics of language.

How New Words are Created

An examination of recently created lexical items—*smog*, *spaceship*, *laundromat*, for example—reveals an astonishing fact. These words are not 'new' but old. They are either old words borrowed from another language or dialect, or they are old elements in novel combinations. The number of words 'made up' out of nothing, such as Lewis Carrol's *jabberwocky* or Edward Lear's *pobble*, are extremely rare—and even these conform to the normal syllabic structure of the language (see Chapter 5).

Methods of creating new lexical items can be assigned to two main classes: items created from **resources within the language** and **borrowing** (these two are sometimes combined).

Items Created from Internal Resources

The following methods of forming new items are important in English:

1. **Affixation** (This is very common.)

    New words can be created by adding prefixes, such as *de-*, *self-*, *anti-* (*desensitise*, *self-service*, *antifreeze*), or suffixes, such as *-ise*, *-ist*, *-able* (*transistorise*, *racialist*, *getatable*).

2. **Analogy**

    e.g. *motorway* after *railway*
    laundromat after *automat*.

3. **Blends** (or **Contamination**)

    Blends occur when two existing words are combined into one new one. They are sometimes called 'portmanteau' words, after the statement of Humpty-Dumpty in *Alice Through the Looking Glass:* 'You see it's like a portmanteau—there are two meanings packed up into one word'.

    e.g. *smog* < *smoke* and *fog*
    brunch < *breakfast* and *lunch*.

4. **Compounds** (This is very common.)

    Two existing words are sometimes juxtaposed to form a new compound lexical item:
    e.g. *bubble car*
    spaceship
    frogman.

5. **Shortening**

    Short words are formed from long ones:
    e.g. *pub* < *public house*
    pram < *perambulator*
    bus < *omnibus*.

6. Acronyms

Acronyms are formed by combining the initial letters of a number of words:

e.g. *radar* < *r*adio *d*etection *a*nd *r*anging
posh < *p*ort *o*ut *s*tarboard *h*ome (in order to get shade from the sun, first-class passengers on a return trip from England to India had port cabins on the outward journey, and starboard ones on the homeward).

7. Conversion

Conversion is the transfer of a word from one word class to another:

e.g. *to garage* < *garage* (verb from noun)
hair-do < *do one's hair*, *have one's hair done* (noun from verb).

8. Folk etymology

Popular misinterpretations of words can sometimes lead to the formation of a new one. The word *groom* originally meant 'boy, lad, servant'. It was popularly linked up with the second element in *bryd-guma* 'espoused man'—and a new word *bridegroom* was formed.

Borrowings (Loanwords)

Lexical items can be borrowed from **within** the language, from another dialect or register (register = specialised social usage, see Chapter 13), or from **outside.**

Internal borrowings frequently start out as slang, which later becomes accepted, such as the words *snob*, *squabble*, *hard up*. *Bird*, now becoming acceptable in the meaning of 'girl', is a northern form of the word 'bride'. *Brass tacks* (= facts) is Cockney rhyming slang. And *jazz* is in origin a slang word from New Orleans which, according to one theory, meant 'sexual intercourse' and was then transferred to the type of music normally played while this was taking place.

A common type of internal borrowing is the adoption of proper names, as the word *sandwich* from Lord Sandwich, the first person to eat his meat between two slices of bread. When used as a verb, this is also an example of conversion.

External borrowings can be 'learned' borrowings from dead languages, e.g. *telephone*, *thermodynamics* from ancient Greek. Such words are usually consciously formed and adopted. Or they can be from a modern language, e.g. *cliché*, *boutique* from French.

An interesting variation is the *calque* or 'loan translation'. Calque means a 'tracing' and is a lexical item whose elements have been directly translated from one language to another. We have borrowed the German word *Wunschdenken*, but translated it into *wishful thinking*. The French have borrowed the word *skyscraper*, but translated it into *gratte-ciel*.

QUESTIONS

1. What is **analogy**?
2. What is a **back formation**?
3. Give an account of some internal reasons for loss of lexical items.
4. Why is it useless to treat changes of meaning in isolation?
5. Give an account of some methods by which new lexical items are created.
6. What is an **acronym**?

PART FOUR

SOME RECENT DEVELOPMENTS

I find my position as an articulate mammal
  bewildering and awesome
Would to God I were a tender apple blawssom.

Ogden Nash

CHAPTER 13

Psycholinguistics and Sociolinguistics

Psycholinguistics and sociolinguistics are two areas of study which have recently become very popular.

These areas overlap, and boundaries between them are difficult to define.

Sometimes, psycholinguistics is defined as **language and the mind,** and sociolinguistics as **language and the community.** Alternatively, psycholinguistics can be said to deal with language and the individual, and sociolinguistics with language and society.

Such distinctions, though obviously oversimplified, are useful as a guide.

Psycholinguistics

Psycholinguistics is of interest to at least three types of people: neurologists, experimental psychologists and linguists. Each approaches the field in a different way.

Neurologists are concerned (among other things) with trying to locate speech mechanisms within the brain. Is there any particular area which deals with speech? If so, is it located in approximately the same place in all individuals, or does it vary from person to person?

So far, all attempts at pinpointing speech areas have proved highly controversial, since conclusions have necessarily been drawn from patients with damaged brains—stroke or accident victims, or epileptics. It is too dangerous to experiment with the brain of a healthy person. And abnormal brains may not accurately reflect the working of normal ones.

Experimental psychologists have a different approach. They devise and carry out experiments in order to discover how the brain organises language, how it stores words, how sentences are planned and so on.

Perhaps the most widely publicised experiments in recent years are those which have attempted to test whether the language planning processes in the brain resemble a transformational grammar. George Miller of Harvard University conducted some early experiments of this type. His results were encouraging. Working on the 1957 version of transformational grammar (see Chapter 8), he found that the time taken to process 'kernel' sentences was shorter than that needed for sentences which included optional transformations such as passive, negative and interrogative. And that the time taken to process two transformations, such as a passive and a negative, was equivalent to the sum of the time it took to process each transformation separately.

This suggested strongly that the brain worked by generating a kernel sentence on which optional transformations were then performed—that is, a sentence such as 'The ball was hit by John' appeared to be produced in two stages. Firstly, a kernel 'John hit the ball' was generated. Secondly, a transformation converted it into 'The ball was hit by John'.

But these early results appear to be contradicted by more recent experiments, and the whole idea is in a state of uncertainty.

Linguists differ from psychologists in that their work is traditionally based more on data collection and observation than on experimentation. It is in the study of child language acquisition that this has proved most useful for psycholinguistics.

The recent awakening of interest in language acquisition is due to a large extent to ideas suggested by transformational grammar.

Child Language Acquisition

Few people in the 1950s queried the processes by which language was acquired. Most assumed that children imitated the adults around them, and that their speech gradually became more accurate as it moved closer to the models they were copying. There seemed to be little mystery attached to this apparently straightforward process.

But Chomsky and his followers drew attention to several interesting points—points that are so obvious that they had been overlooked in many previous studies.

Firstly, children acquire language in a remarkably short time. The major part of acquisition is crammed into approximately eighteen months (eighteenth–thirty-sixth month). And all children, even relatively stupid ones, do this seemingly effortlessly and competently.

Secondly, adult speech is the only apparent source of data from which a child works in achieving this mammoth task. Yet adult speech is extremely confusing. There are numerous unfinished sentences and ungrammatical utterances. How do children extract a grammar from this jumble?

According to some modern scholars, children must be born with some innate knowledge of the properties of language. They acquire language so easily and so fast because they know, in outline, what it is they have to learn. Every child has a 'blueprint' of language universals in his brain. All he has to do is to discover how his own language fits into these universal patterns. In transformational terms, a child has an innate knowledge of universal deep structures. All he has to learn are the relevant transformations for converting this deep structure into the surface structure realisation of his own language.

For example, a suggestion put forward at one stage was that children have an innate understanding of the relationship between subject and predicate:

e.g. SUBJECT   PREDICATE

Mary   is tired
Daddy   is going in the car

So child utterances such as *Mary tired* and *Daddy car* could be interpreted as conforming to this elementary pattern.

Such suggestions have generated an immense amount of controversy. And, more important, a significant amount of research.

No detailed solution has yet been found to the question, 'What kind of innate knowledge is a child born with?'. But a greater understanding of the nature of language is slowly being achieved as a result of the ensuing research.

Two points in particular have become clearer. Firstly, language has all the characteristics of **maturationally controlled behaviour.** Secondly, child language is **rule governed** at every stage.

Language as Maturationally Controlled Behaviour

It used to be thought that animal behaviour could be divided into two types: that which was inborn and natural (e.g. dogs naturally bark), and that which was learned and unnatural (e.g. dogs can be taught to beg).

Recent work has shown that this division is by no means clear-cut and may be misleading.

Many types of behaviour develop 'naturally' at a certain age, provided that the surrounding environment is adequate and teaching is available at the crucial time.

Such behaviour is **maturationally controlled.** Arguments as to whether it is inborn or learnt are futile. Both nature and nurture are important. Innate potentialities lay down the framework. Within this framework, there is wide variation depending on the environment.

From the age of around eighteen months, human infants are in a state of 'language readiness'. The urge for language to emerge at this time is very strong, and only very extraordinary circumstances will suppress it. (A child brought up in complete isolation will not acquire language.) But all normal children—and some abnormal ones—will begin to speak if they hear language going on around them at this time.

Rule-governed Nature of Child Grammar

Child grammar is **rule governed** at every stage. It is never at any time a haphazard selection or substandard version of adult speech, but is always a complete grammar with rules of its own. The system will be simpler than that of an adult, but nevertheless it will be complete.

Two-word utterances of the type *bye bye dada, want milk, that shoe*, for example, are not just casual juxtapositions of words, but are carefully structured.

In terms of a grammar, two different word classes are recognisable. (Word classes are discussed in Chapter 6.) These will not, of course, conform to adult word classes:

CLASS 1	CLASS 2
bye bye	dada
want	milk
that	shoe
	mama
	car, etc.

Class 1 contains a relatively small number of words which never occur by themselves and which are always found in the same position in an utterance. Such a word class is sometimes referred to as a **pivot** class.

Class 2 contains a much larger number of words which may also occur by themselves as single-word utterances.

As a child gets older, its grammar will get more complex, but similar underlying patterns will always be detectable.

Another more advanced but obvious example of the rule-governed nature of child language are forms such as *mans*, *foots*, *gooses*, which children produce frequently. Such plurals occur even when a child understands and responds correctly to the adult forms *men*, *feet*, *geese*. This is proof that a child's own rules of grammar are more important to him than mere imitation.

Future Prospects

Most recent studies of child language have paid great attention to the child's utterances and far too little to the speech of its parents.

There are signs that this obsession with the child alone is beginning to pass. The realisation is growing that future studies must take into account the child's whole environment, and particularly the speech of its parents.

Roger Brown and Ursula Bellugi of Harvard University have noted an interesting type of interaction which takes place between parent and child, two processes which they call 'imitation and reduction' and 'imitation and expansion'.

They noted that a child tends to imitate its mother, but reduces the utterance in length and omits inflections, resulting in a 'telegraphic' style of speech:

> Mother: Daddy's going in the car.
> Child: Daddy car.

Conversely, a parent tends to imitate the child by repeating and expanding its utterances:

Child: Daddy car.
Mother: Yes, that's right, Daddy's going in the car.

But larger samples of parent and child speech must be studied before any firm conclusions about universal acquisition processes are reached.

Other Areas of Psycholinguistics

Psycholinguistics covers a wide range of interests, and numerous other aspects are currently being studied.

The study of speech disturbances is a promising area of research. Major types of speech impairment (resulting from head injuries and strokes) and minor slips of the tongue (observable in normal people) can both provide useful clues to the processes involved in the planning and production of speech.

Pausing and hesitations can also provide clues to these processes. Pausing, though usually unnoticed in normal conversation, can sometimes take up as much as half the speaking time. And complexity of thought processes seem likely to be correlated with the length of the pauses.

Another facet of psycholinguistics (which overlaps with sociolinguistics) is the attempt to gauge how language affects the way we perceive the world.

Each language splits up the world in different ways. To what extent does this affect the speakers of the language? For example, does a man whose language has the same word for both *mauve* and *purple* find it more difficult to distinguish between these colours than a man whose language separates them?

Experiments indicate that the answer is a tentative 'yes'—though much more research needs to be done.

Sociolinguists study this phenomenon for a slightly different reason. They try to find out to what extent language influences social attitudes. Does a man who refers to his girl friend as his *dolly* or his *bird* have less respect for women than one who refers to her as his *fiancée*, for example?

Sociolinguistics

Perhaps the first question that a sociolinguist asks is, 'What is a language?'.

Is 'a language' a useful linguistic notion? Can it be defined geographically? Can it be equated with nationality? Or should a language be defined by the mutual intelligibility of its speakers?

The answer to all these questions appears to be 'no'.

A geographical definition of a language would separate Australian, British and American English, which is obviously unsatisfactory.

'Nationality' is a vague notion which has little to do with the language a man speaks. Numerous Soviet Jews, for example, regard themselves as essentially Jewish, yet speak Russian.

Mutual intelligibility is of little help, since a Yorkshireman and a Cornishman are likely to find it harder to understand one another than a Welshman and a Breton onion seller.

And there is no objective linguistic criterion which can be applied. Dutch and German are normally regarded as separate languages, yet they are structurally more alike than some of the so-called dialects of Chinese.

Faced with this dilemma, sociolinguists prefer to start with the notion of a **speech community** rather than a 'language'. And they define a speech community as any group of people who consider that they speak a single language.

Consequently, Dutch and German must be regarded as separate languages, since, in spite of their similarities, the Dutch consider they speak Dutch and the Germans consider they speak German. And all the Chinese dialects must be classified as one language, because, in spite of far-reaching differences, their speakers all consider they speak Chinese.

Speech Varieties

Within a speech community, there is considerable variation. The speech of its members varies according to geographical location, age, occupation and social class. This variation frequently reflects social attitudes which go far beyond language. So the study of speech varieties is perhaps the most important aspect of sociolinguistics.

The most obvious type of variety in a speech community is the use of different **dialects.**

A dialect is usually associated with a **particular** geographical area, such as the Lancashire and Cockney dialects of English, which are spoken in Lancashire and London respectively.

The term **dialect** refers to a far greater difference than mere pronunciation. 'Don't ee go an get drownded in Thirlmere: yon's used for drinkin water' (Lancashire) differs from standard British English in sound system, grammar and vocabulary. American English ranks as a different dialect from British English, with phonological innovations such as nasal vowels, and constructions such as 'I kinda figured maybe' and 'He said for you not to worry'.

Unfortunately, in everyday usage, the technical term dialect is often confused with the word **accent.**

An accent refers only to a difference in pronunciation. A Yorkshireman and a Londoner are likely to speak English with different accents. But if the underlying grammar and vocabulary are the same, they will be speaking the same dialect. In fact, although a considerable number of local accents are still found in Britain, dialects are dying out, due to the influence of education, radio and television.

Register

Another important type of language variety is **register.** This refers to the many styles and specialised usages within a language.

Each person normally speaks only one dialect, but he is likely to be in command of several registers, which he varies according to the situation.

For example, the same person might utter any of the following three sentences, depending on where he was:

1. 'I should be grateful if you would make less noise.'
2. 'Please be quiet.'
3. 'Shut up.'

Registers of this type, which refer to the **style of discourse,** can be classified on a scale ranging from **high** (or **formal**) to **low** (or **informal**).

Humour sometimes depends on the use of an inappropriate style of discourse:

'Scintillate, scintillate, diminutive asteroid,
How I speculate as to your identity'

seems amusing because of the use of a formal register to 'translate' a nursery rhyme associated with an informal register ('Twinkle, twinkle, little star . . .').

But register does not only apply to degrees of formality. It can also refer to the **field of discourse**, the specialised language of an activity or an occupation.

Every field of discourse has its own register. 'Love-forty', 'advantage server', 'game, set and match' all belong to the language of tennis. 'Beloved brethren, we are gathered together . . .' to church. 'Hallo operator, I can't get dialling tone' to the language of phone conversations. 'Fantastic reductions! Prices slashed!' to sales.

Sociolinguists attempt to correlate registers with their social settings or **contexts of situation.** This may have interesting implications, since language is often a useful mirror of social attitudes.

Style of discourse, for example, can sometimes be correlated with class distinctions. According to Basil Bernstein of London University, English working-class families tend to use a type of language that is informal and elliptical. Middle-class families use language that is more formal and more explicit. Working-class 'Scram' or 'Shut your trap', for example, might be expressed as 'Please go away, I'm trying to work' or 'Stop talking and eat up your breakfast' in a middle-class household.

As a result, Bernstein suggests that working-class children may be at an educational disadvantage because of their impoverished language background.

Bilingualism and Language Planning

Another facet of sociolinguistics is **language contact** situations: the study of communities where more than one language is in everyday use.

In such communities, a switch in register may be marked by a switch in language, as in the saying attributed to the Holy Roman Emperor Charles V: 'I speak Spanish to God, Italian to women, French to men and German to my horse'.

Different languages are (perhaps unconsciously) assigned to different styles and fields of discourse. One language may be used in the home for addressing women and children. Another language may be used by men talking in the pub. And another may be used for formal situations, such as a law suit.

This has important implications for **language planning,** when a government wishes to impose a language on a community for political reasons.

Such a programme stands a greater chance of success if it has been preceded by a study of the uses of the language to be imposed. Ideally, new uses of this language should be gradually grafted onto existing ones. This is likely to be more satisfactory than a sudden arbitrary switch to one language for all registers.

A further aspect of language contact situations is the study of **mixed languages**—languages whose phonology, grammar and vocabulary have become merged with that of another. Such languages are usually called **creoles** if they achieve full status as an independent language (such as Creole French in Mauritius, which is acquired by children as a first language). Mixed languages which are restricted to certain uses are known as **pidgins.**

QUESTIONS

1. What is meant by **maturationally controlled behaviour?**
2. Child language is **rule governed** at every stage. Explain.
3. What is a **speech community?**
4. Distinguish between **dialects** and **registers.**
5. Distinguish between **pidgins** and **creoles.**

The Phonemes of British English
and some important allophones

'Received pronunciation' (R.P.), or educated Southern British English, sometimes equated with 'B.B.C. English'.

PHONEME	ALLOPHONES	EXAMPLES
/p/	[pʰ]	*p*ill
	[p]	s*p*ill
/b/	[b]	*b*ill
/t/	[tʰ]	*t*ill
	[t]	s*t*ill
/d/	[d]	*d*ale
/k/	[cʰ]	*k*ill
	[c]	s*k*ill
	[kʰ]	*c*orn
	[k]	s*c*orn
/g/	[ɟ]	*g*et
	[g]	*g*ot
/m/	[m]	*m*ake

/n/	[n]	*n*ame
/ŋ/	[ŋ]	ra*ng*
/l/	[l]	*l*amb
	[ł]	fu*ll*
/r/	[r]	*r*am
	[ɹ]	
/f/	[f]	*f*ish
/v/	[v]	*v*ase
/θ/	[θ]	*th*in
/ð/	[ð]	*th*en
/s/	[s]	*s*o
/z/	[z]	*z*oo
/ʃ/	[ʃ]	*sh*oe
/ʒ/	[ʒ]	bei*g*e
/h/	[h]	*h*ot
/tʃ/	[tʃ]	*ch*in
/dʒ/	[dʒ]	*j*am
/w/	[w]	*w*ood
/j/	[j]	*y*et
[iː]	[iː]	b*ea*t
/ɪ/	[ɪ]	b*i*t
/e/	[e]	b*e*t

/æ/	[æ]	b*a*t
/ɑː/	[ɑː]	h*ea*rt
/uː/	[uː]	b*oo*t
/ʊ/	[ʊ]	p*u*t
/ɔː/	[ɔː]	p*o*rt
/ɒ/	[ɒ]	p*o*t
/ʌ/	[ʌ]	b*u*t
/ɜː/	[ɜː]	b*i*rd
/ə/	[ə]	sof*a*
/eɪ/	[eɪ]	p*ay*
/aɪ/	[aɪ]	p*ie*
/ɔɪ/	[ɔɪ]	b*oy*
/aʊ/	[aʊ]	h*ow*
/əʊ/	[əʊ]	b*oa*t
/ɪə/	[ɪə]	p*ier*
/ɛə/	[ɛə]	p*ear*
/ʊə/	[ʊə]	p*oor*

For a fuller account, see A. C. Gimson, *An Introduction to the Pronunciation of English* (Arnold, 2nd edition 1970).

Phonetics: The Study of Speech Sounds

Speech sounds may be described and classified mainly in two ways:

(i) in **articulatory** terms (i.e. means of production)
(ii) in **acoustic** terms (i.e. analysis of sound waves).

The following brief descriptions are all **articulatory.**

Consonants and Vowels

The traditional distinction between consonantal-type sounds and vowel-type sounds is a useful one (though closer analysis shows that it is not as clear-cut or as easy to define as appears at first sight).

English Consonants

English consonantal sounds are those which are most easily described in terms of three variables:

(i) **voicing**
(ii) **place of articulation**
(iii) **manner of articulation.**

Voicing

The vocal cords are thin strips of membrane in the throat (see Figure 1). If they vibrate as a sound is produced, it is said to be **voiced,** as in the production of [b d g v ð z ʒ dʒ m n ŋ l r w j]. This vibration can be felt if a hand is placed on the outside of the throat as the sound is uttered. If the vocal cords do not vibrate as a sound is produced, it is said to be **voiceless,** as in [p t k f θ s ʃ tʃ].

Place of Articulation

The **place of articulation** describes the point at which the articulators actually touch, or are at their closest. The most important places for the production of English sounds are listed in the table below. See also Figure 1.

	ARTICULATORS	*EXAMPLES*
BILABIAL	Upper lip + lower lip	[p b m w]
DENTAL	Teeth + tongue	[θ ð]
LABIO-DENTAL	Lower lip + upper teeth	[f v]
ALVEOLAR	Alveolar (teeth) ridge + tongue	[t d s z r l n]
PALATO-ALVEOLAR	Join of hard palate and alveolar ridge + tongue	[ʃ ʒ tʃ dʒ]
PALATAL	Hard palate + tongue	[j c ɟ]
VELAR	Soft palate + tongue	[k g]
GLOTTAL	Vocal cords	[h]

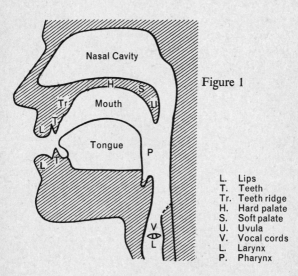

Figure 1

L. Lips
T. Teeth
Tr. Teeth ridge
H. Hard palate
S. Soft palate
U. Uvula
V. Vocal cords
L. Larynx
P. Pharynx

Manner of Articulation

The **manner of articulation** describes the type of obstruction caused by the narrowing or closure of the articulators.

	MOVEMENT OF ARTICULATORS	*EXAMPLES*
STOP	Complete closure	[p b t d k g]
AFFRICATE	Closure, then slow separation	[tʃ dʒ]
FRICATIVE	Narrowing, resulting in audible friction	[f v θ ð s z]
NASAL	Complete closure in mouth, air escapes through nose	[m n ŋ]
ROLL	Rapid intermittent closures	[r]
LATERAL	Closure in centre of mouth, air escapes down sides	[l]
SEMIVOWELS AND FRICTIONLESS CONTINUANT	Slight narrowing, not enough to cause friction	[w j ɹ]

Identification of Sounds

Any English sound can be described and identified in the above terms:

> e.g. [s] is a **voiceless alveolar fricative**
> [b] is a **voiced bilabial stop**
> [tʃ] is a **voiceless palato-alveolar affricate.**

This information can also be conveniently plotted on a chart (Figure 2).

Note that the information above is by no means a complete phonetic description. It represents the minimum necessary for distinguishing between English consonantal-type phonemes in articulatory terms.

	BILABIAL	LABIO-DENTAL	DENTAL	ALVEOLAR	PALATO-ALVEOLAR	PALATAL	VELAR	GLOTTAL
STOP vless	p			t		c	k	
STOP vd	b			d		ɟ	g	
AFFRICATE vless					tʃ			
AFFRICATE vd					dʒ			
FRICATIVE vless		f	θ	s	ʃ			h
FRICATIVE vd		v	ð	z	ʒ			
NASAL	m			n			ŋ	
LATERAL				l			ɫ	
ROLL				r				
SEMIVOWEL AND FRICTIONLESS CONTINUANT	w			ɹ		j		

Figure 2

Notes

Notes on other phonetic terms and symbols used in the text relating to consonants:

1. **Sibilant.** A general term used to denote 'hissing' sounds, e.g. [s z].
2. **Liquid.** A general term used to cover [l] and [r].
3. **Frictionless continuant.** A term used to describe [ɹ], the frictionless variant of the phoneme /r/ which is commonly used in R.P. (The rolled variety of /r/ is more frequent in Scotland.)
4. **Syllabic nasals,** [m̩] [n̩] Nasal consonants which constitute a whole syllable, as in *bottom* [bɒtm̩], *button* [bʌtn̩].

English Vowels

Vowel-type sounds are those in which the sound depends mainly on variations in the position of the tongue. They are normally voiced. English (British) vowel-type sounds are most easily described in terms of two variables:[1]

  (i) **height of the tongue**
 (ii) **part of the tongue** which is raised or lowered.

Various tongue positions within the mouth can be seen in Figure 3.

---

[1] In the description of vowels, **lip-rounding** is usually added as a third variable. But in British English, front and central vowels are automatically unrounded, and back vowels (except [ɑ:]) are automatically rounded. So this distinction has been omitted. Note, however, that in describing French and German vowels lip-rounding is a major variable.

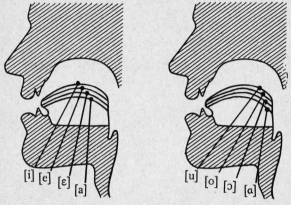

Figure 3

In the figure,

[i] shows the tongue at its highest and farthest forward

[a] shows the tongue at its lowest and farthest forward

[u] shows the tongue at its highest and farthest back

[ɑ] shows the tongue at its lowest and farthest back.

These extremes are represented on the diagram below:

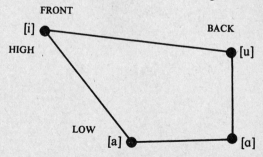

Between these extreme four points, [e] and [ε] are marked equidistant between [i] and [a], and [o] and [ɔ] are marked equidistant between [u] and [ɑ].

These eight points were called the **cardinal vowels** by Daniel Jones, and the vowels of any language are usually plotted onto this quadrangle.

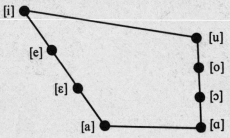

Note that sometimes for speed and diagrammatic purposes vowels are plotted on a **triangle,** which is derived from the cardinal vowel figure.

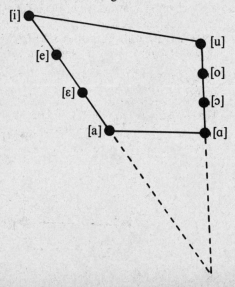

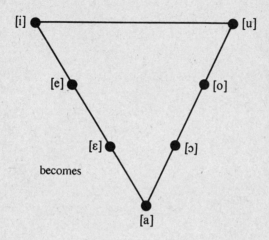

English vowel sounds are of two types:

(i) relatively **pure,** or unchanging vowels, as in *set, sat, sit*
(ii) **diphthongs,** or gliding vowels, as in *boat, bite, boil*, in which the tongue position alters as the sound is made.

The **pure vowels** are fairly easy to plot on the cardinal vowel diagram (though the placing is only approximate owing to the large amount of variation found in British vowel sounds). Two dots beside a vowel indicate **length,** e.g. [uː].

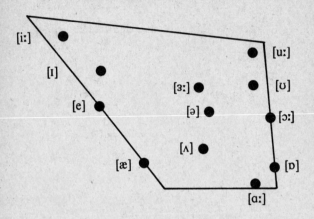

A less accurate, but useful schematic diagram, is as follows:

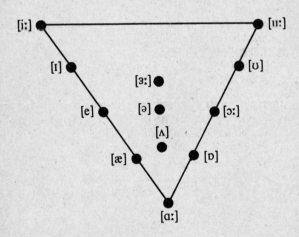

Diphthongs are shown by arrows linking the tongue positions:

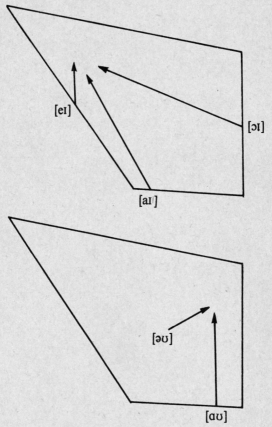

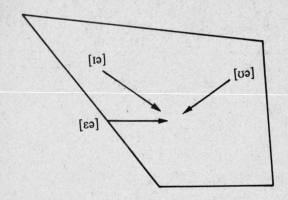

Reading Suggestions for Phonetics

D. Abercrombie, *Elements of General Phonetics* (Edinburgh 1967).

J. D. O'Connor, *Phonetics* (Pelican 1971).

A. C. Gimson, *An Introduction to the Pronunciation of English* (Arnold 2nd edition 1970).

The Principles of the International Phonetic Association. (Booklet obtainable from the Secretary of the International Phonetics Association, Department of Phonetics, University College, London, W.C.1.)

J. C. Wells and G. Colson, *Practical Phonetics* (Pitman, 1971).

Table of Symbols

[ ]	used for phonetic transcription
/ /	used for phonemic transcription
{ }	used to denote morphemes
*	indicates a reconstructed form
	or an ungrammatical expression
→	means 'rewrite as'
>	means 'changed into'

Suggestions for Further Reading
(in alphabetical order)

A. ELEMENTARY

D. Bolinger, *Aspects of Language* (Harcourt, Brace & World 1968). A stimulating but sometimes confusing general introduction.

Y. R. Chao, *Language and Symbolic Systems* (Cambridge University Press 1968). A brief, clear and useful introduction.

D. Crystal, *Linguistics* (Pelican 1971). A general survey of present-day linguistics.

R. W. Langacker, *Language and its Structure* (Harcourt, Brace & World 1967). An introduction written from the point of view of transformational grammar.

F. Palmer, *Grammar* (Pelican 1971). A clear and useful discussion of traditional grammatical concepts, and their relevance to current-day linguistics.

B. BASIC TEXT BOOKS

H. A. Gleason, *Introduction to Descriptive Linguistics* (Holt, Rinehart, Winston, revised edition 1961). A useful, straightforward book, now slightly out of date. Emphasis is on a practical rather than a theoretical approach, with English as the language of exemplification. (Unfortunately both phonetic symbols and pronunciation follow American rather than British usage.)

C. F. Hockett, *A Course in Modern Linguistics* (New York: Macmillan 1958). A thorough but often turgid approach to the subject, somewhat out of date.

J. Lyons, *Introduction to Theoretical Linguistics* (Cambridge

University Press 1968). Insightful and stimulating. Difficult to read in places, but worth the effort.

A. Martinet, *Elements of General Linguistics* (Faber & Faber 1964). A clear introduction, particularly useful for views on language change. Terminology occasionally differs from English and American usage.

R. H. Robins, *General Linguistics: an Introductory Survey* (Longmans, second edition 1971). A general coverage of the subject, including useful passages on Firthian theory.

C. TRANSFORMATIONAL–GENERATIVE GRAMMAR

M. K. Burt, *From Deep to Surface Structure: An Introduction to Transformational Syntax* (Holt, Rinehart & Winston 1971). A valuable and stimulating book, to be used to supplement a more basic course.

N. Chomsky, *Syntactic Structures* (Mouton 1957). Transformational grammar, original version.

N. Chomsky, *Aspects of the Theory of Syntax* (MIT Press 1965). Transformational grammar, revised version. Difficult to read.

R. Fowler, *An Introduction to Transformational Syntax* (Routledge & Kegan Paul 1971). A useful, elementary textbook.

R. A. Jacobs & P. S. Rosenbaum, *English Transformational Grammar* (Blaisdell 1968). A useful book, though tends to be vague in places.

R. D. King, *Historical Linguistics and Generative Grammar* (Prentice-Hall 1969). A treatment of historical linguistics within the framework of transformational grammar.

M. Lester, *Introductory Transformational Grammar of English* (Holt, Rinehart & Winston 1971). Perhaps the most useful of the elementary text books for people working by themselves. Clear, step-by-step presentation.

B. L. Liles, *An Introductory Transformational Grammar* (Prentice-Hall 1971). Another useful elementary text book.

J. Lyons, *Chimsky* (Fontana 1970). A useful guide to *Syntactic Structures*.

D. CLASSICS

L. Bloomfield, *Language* (Allen & Unwin 1935). The 'father' of American descriptive linguistics. Many text books are, consciously or unconsciously, based on his work.

J. R. Firth, *The Tongues of Men and Speech* (Oxford University Press 1964 reprint). A former Professor of General Linguistics at London University, Firth is regarded as the founder of the 'London school' of linguistics.

E. Sapir, *Language* (Harcourt, Brace & World 1921). American anthropologist-linguist-sociologist. Noted for his insights into language patterning, and his treatment of language against a broad cultural background.

F. de Saussure, *Course in General Linguistics* (New York: Philosophical Library 1959). A Swiss scholar, one of the first scholars to realise the interdependence of linguistic units. Has profoundly influenced European linguistics.

E. OTHER USEFUL BOOKS

F. P. Dinneen, *An Introduction to General Linguistics* (Holt, Rinehart & Winston 1967). A useful, semi-historical approach to linguistic theory, comparing the contributions of various 'schools'.

J. A. Fishman, *Sociolinguistics: A Brief Introduction* (Newbury House 1970). One of the few surveys of sociolinguistics on the market.

M. A. K. Halliday, A. McIntosh & P. Strevens, *The Linguistic Sciences and Language Teaching* (Longmans 1965). A stimulating but idiosyncratic approach to linguistic theory, with a useful section on language teaching.

W. P. Lehmann, *Historical Linguistics: An Introduction* (Holt, Rinehart & Winston 1962). One of the few surveys of historical linguistics available. Fairly old-fashioned in outlook.

R. Lord, *Teach Yourself Comparative Linguistics* (English Universities Press 1966). Covers several areas of linguistics omitted in the current book, e.g. survey of languages of the world.

J. Lyons (ed.), *New Horizons in Linguistics* (Penguin 1970). A patchy book, which requires a fair knowledge of linguistics. Some stimulating articles, but useful above all for its extensive and up-to-date bibliography.

D. I. Slobin, *Psycholinguistics* (Scott, Foresman 1971). A brief and useful survey.

F. LINGUISTICS PERIODICALS

There are numerous linguistics periodicals, of which the following are perhaps the best known:

International Journal of American Linguistics (Baltimore).
Journal of Linguistics (London).
Language (Baltimore).
Lingua (Amsterdam).
Linguistic Inquiry (Cambridge, Mass.).
Linguistics (The Hague).
Word (New York).